History of the
Iowa Automobile Dealers Association

History of the Iowa Automobile Dealers Association. Copyright ©2008 by The Iowa Automobile Dealers Association. Printed in United States. All rights reserved. No part of this book may be reproduced in any form or by any electronic or mechanical means including information storage and retrieval systems without permission in writing from the publisher, except by a reviewer who may quote brief passages in a review. Published by Iowa Automobile Dealers Association, 1111 Office Park Road, West Des Moines, IA 50265. First edition.

Library of Congress Cataloging-in-Publication Data

Schoffner, Pam.
History of the Iowa Automobile Dealers Association/by Pam Schoffner.
p. cm.
ISBN 0-615-22574-8

Editing/Proofing: Deb Engle, GoldenTree Communications
and Lisa Kingsley, Waterbury Publications, Inc.

Design: Cooper Smith & Company

Table of Contents

Introduction 5

The Road Taken...6

The 1920s..12

The 1930s..20

The 1940s..30

The 1950s..44

The 1960s..52

The 1970s..62

The 1980s..72

The 1990s..82

The 2000s..94

Past Presidents and Board Chairmen of IADA...............................104

IADA Staff Leaders...105

Presidents' Stories..106

TIME Magazine's Quality Dealer Award Recipients from Iowa............108

Hall of Fame instituted in 2008..109

IADA Hall of Fame..110

Acknowledgements...112

Dedicated to
M.O. "Bud" Kahn, IADA president in 1961,
who made sure IADA friendships, accomplishments,
and memories are captured and held in the heart.

Introduction

The idea of compiling the Iowa Automobile Dealers Association history began 25 years ago with my predecessor, Al Kahl. When Al retired in 1982, he considered taking on the project but faced the inevitable question, "Where do you start?" The idea had the support of M.O. "Bud" Kahn, IADA president in 1961, who was adamant that we capture the creation and evolution of IADA before the stories were lost.

In 2005—two years after Al's death—I invited Pam Schoffner, an Iowa writer with a background in association work, to listen to our past presidents and chairman for an afternoon as they shared their favorite association memories. As luck would have it, Pam was hooked by the camaraderie of a room full of competitors and returned the next morning to learn more.

We sent Pam back to her office with five large boxes that contained every association newsletter dating back to 1919. It took nearly two years to compile the history and an additional six months to secure photos and related stories from dealers and their families.

The history section is based entirely on the newsletters—the information the association staff put in print to its members through the years. Unless otherwise noted, all quoted material is from these newsletters. No attempt was made to prove or disprove information by additional research. The history stands as it was originally told.

My thanks go to Iowa automobile dealers—past and present—who gave their energy, ideas, friendship, and unending commitment to make IADA the solid association it is today. You wrote quite a story.

Gary W. Thomas
IADA President

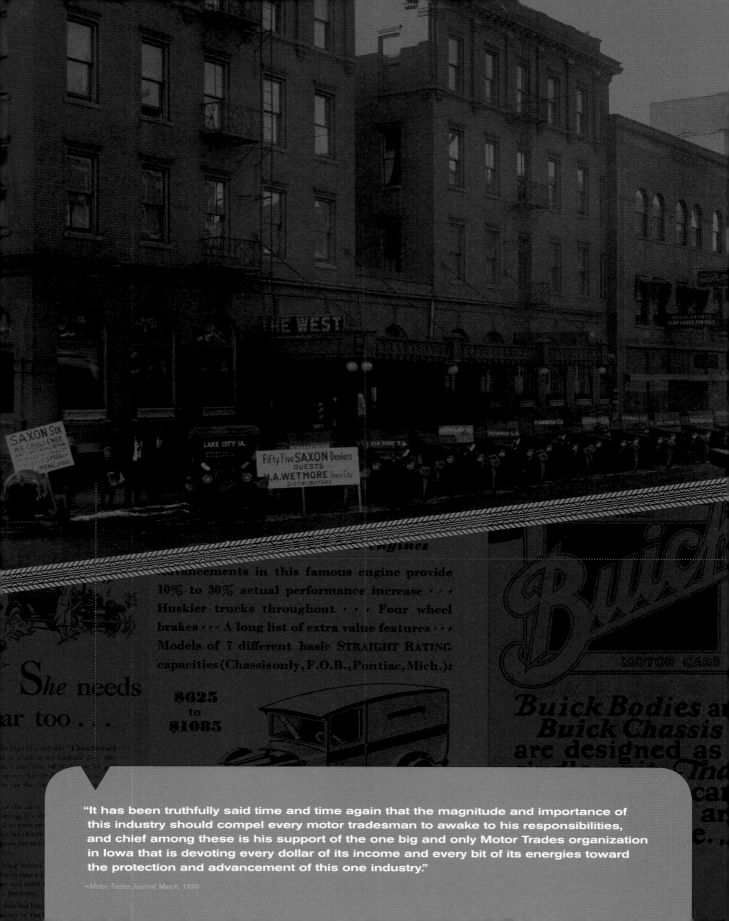

THE WEST

SAXON SIX
WE CHALLENGE
ANY CAR IN ITS
PRICE CLASS
SPEED
...

LAKE CITY IA.

Fifty Five SAXON Dealers
GUESTS
H.A.WETMORE Sioux City
DISTRIBUTORS

ELK POINT S.D.

STORM LAKE IA.

HOWARD S.D.

engines

vancements in this famous engine provide
10% to 30% actual performance increase · · ·
Huskier trucks throughout · · · Four wheel
brakes · · · A long list of extra value features · · ·
Models of 7 different basic STRAIGHT RATING
capacities (Chassis only, F.O.B., Pontiac, Mich.):

$625
to
$1085

She needs
ar too . . .

Buick
MOTOR CARS

Buick Bodies ar
Buick Chassis
are designed as

"It has been truthfully said time and time again that the magnitude and importance of
this industry should compel every motor tradesman to awake to his responsibilities,
and chief among these is his support of the one big and only Motor Trades organization
in Iowa that is devoting every dollar of its income and every bit of its energies toward
the protection and advancement of this one industry."

–*Motor Trades Journal*, March, 1920

The Road Taken

On February 15, 1917, 55 Saxon dealers, the guests of H.A (Harry) Wetmore, gathered at the West Hotel in Sioux City. The sign at left reads: "Saxon Six—We challenge any car owned within 150 miles of Sioux City for any kind of speed or climbing contest." Wetmore raced his automobiles to promote speed and reliability, and he drove a Saxon in the first Pikes Peak Hill Climb in 1916, a race that is still held each year. Between 1908 when he moved to Sioux City and 1938, Wetmore sold 24 different makes of automobiles, plus Excelsior Motorcycles and Waterloo Boy and Wetmore tractors, both at retail and as a distributor to other dealers in the Midwest.

I In 1919, World War I had just ended. The United States was readjusting. And the automobile industry was called "the largest single industry in the great commonwealth of Iowa."

Iowans involved in motor trades were looking toward the Thirty-Eighth General Assembly in hopes that it would pass legislation creating hard-surfaced roads. A well-organized "mud roads gang" had been victorious during the Thirty-Seventh General Assembly that ended April 14, 1917. But engineers and observers back from France were telling how that country's paved roads had "saved Paris in 1914 and enabled Rheims to withstand the onslaught of the Germans for four years." Sentiment had grown favorable to hard-surfaced roads in Iowa, and Iowa's motor trades began mobilizing for statewide road improvement.

Getting Started

During the war, local motor trades organizations had been formed in Sioux City, Fort Dodge, Mason City, Dubuque, Waterloo, Cedar Rapids, Davenport, Clinton, Burlington, Oskaloosa, and Des Moines. These groups

John Hanson

operated independently. John Hanson, Hanson and O'Harrow, Waterloo, was president of the Northeastern Iowa Automobile Dealers Association. Hanson planned to represent the industry during the Thirty-Eighth General Assembly, which opened January 13, 1919, but he determined that the project required a call to "all the larger places of the state." On March 31, 1919, a meeting of "36 serious-minded, far-sighted progressive motor tradesmen" at the Chamber of Commerce Salon in Des Moines prompted the creation of the Iowa Motor Trades Bureau.

Ford automobile showroom and supply shop, approximately 1910.

photo credit State Historical Society of Iowa–Des Moines

Did Iowa's roads need improvement? You bet. Here's Second Avenue of Des Moines in an early photo.

photo credit State Historical Society of Iowa–Des Moines

John Rude

John Rude, Rude Auto Company of Marshalltown, became the first president, with John Hanson serving as vice president. The group elected a treasurer, chose 13 directors, and appointed committees. In the first nine days of April, 1919, the directors held five formal meetings, received reports from several committees, conferred daily with legislators, met with the joint committee of the House and Senate on the proposed motor vehicle bill, elected a secretary, and attended legislative sessions continuously until the highway and motor vehicle laws passed. Within months the bureau had office space—first in the Securities Building and then in the Shops Building—in Des Moines. A stenographer was employed, and a secretary/editor, A.J. "Andy" Knapp, assumed office leadership responsibilities and began publishing a 24-page monthly magazine with industry advertising. Within the first eight months, more than 38,000 pieces of mail were sent from the bureau's office.

Membership

One month after its formation, the bureau had 160 members. Membership dues were set at $5. Fieldwork and the organization of new units of affiliated organizations helped close the first year at 955 active members.

John Rude wrote: "We should not organize for the sole object of influencing legislation or protecting us against some unjust taxation. We must organize not only with this purpose in view, but with a broader idea of putting our individual businesses on a business basis, which means that we should make money and operate our places in a way which will not invite criticism. If we do this, we need not fear but that we will receive just treatment from every source, as all will know that we are able to protect ourselves."

The spirit of cooperation and confidence in one another as motor tradesmen grew within the county groups as 21 affiliated bureaus were created during the first year. The group's magazine stated: "These men get together and discuss matters of common interest, they call each other by their first names, and so great is that spirit of harmony that they visit back and forth, buy from each other, and the members throughout the county vie with each other in attendance at the meetings."

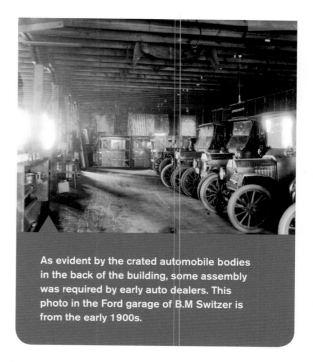

As evident by the crated automobile bodies in the back of the building, some assembly was required by early auto dealers. This photo in the Ford garage of B.M Switzer is from the early 1900s.

The steps of the Iowa Capitol Building provided the location for a demonstration of the "Gearless Carter Car" in Des Moines in 1914. Carter Car was identified as an Iowa company at 1216 Locust Street.

photo credit State Historical Society of Iowa–Des Moines

A 1904 Peerless owned by Charles Denman.

Earlham, Iowa, approximately 1910.

First-Year Accomplishments

During its first year, the bureau helped compile a motor vehicle bill that eliminated much of what motor tradesmen considered "discriminatory" and "unfair handicaps upon any legitimate business." It also secured a provision that permitted car owners to register their motor vehicle with their county treasurer, reduced by about half the license fee for motor trucks, and reduced the price of second and subsequent sets of dealers' number plates from $25 to $15 per set. In 1920, this saved Iowa dealers $20,000 to $30,000 on plates alone.

First Convention

Some 327 motor tradesmen attended the first annual state convention, held November 11–13, 1919, in Des Moines. Members heard about "close cooperation" from the business manager of the National Automobile Dealers Association (NADA), a group they would affiliate with one year later. They also took part in an open discussion on "The Used Car Evil" and heard presentations about the new motor vehicle law, the need for a lien law for motor trades, the value of permanent highways, the motor truck as an economic farm necessity, and business/office management topics.

Participants were disappointed by the cancellation of a program on whether motor tradesmen should sell power-driven farm equipment, but they delighted in the debut of a "National Motor Truck Development Tour in moving pictures" and enjoyed a musical quartet (in "up-to-date motor togs") as well as wrestling and boxing matches that were part of the convention activities. The first gathering even had a ladies' program. Attendees voted a dues increase to $10 that became effective in January, 1920. The entire cost of the convention: $553.58.

Martin Esbeck's Kimballton garage sold Dodge, Velie, and Rio automobiles as early as 1903.

Family AFFAIR

Imagine that you're an auto dealer in the early 1900s, and two of the people you rely on most to help you in business are your teenage daughters. One drives automobiles with you from Chicago to your dealership in Keokuk County, and the other stays at the homes of your customers for weeks at a time to teach them to drive.

Pauline Kitzman Hazen, Louise Kitzman Bos, and Enid Kitzmann Phillips—granddaughters of Frank L. Emery of What Cheer—told their family's story to IADA:

F.L. Emery was a good mechanic and ran a garage when he became a Rambler dealer in What Cheer around 1908. According to Frank's wife, he was the first auto dealer in Keokuk County. Emery's daughter, Zella Emery (later Kitzman), was the first woman driver in Keokuk County. Once a car was purchased—typically by a wealthier family—teenage Zella stayed with the family for a week or two to teach them to drive.

Vera, Zella's sister, accompanied her father on train trips to Chicago to pick up inventory, and the two returned on "White Way Highway" (Highway 6), each driving an automobile back to What Cheer. Pauline recalls her grandmother saying, "Vera only knew one speed, and that was as fast as it would go." Her grandmother also said F.L. Emery borrowed on his life insurance to pay for the dealership's arriving inventory. To help his fellow businessmen keep their doors open, Emery also operated the garage/dealership of the Hemsley brothers when those What Cheer men served in World War I.

To The Public

I have just arrived with two new Nash automobiles from Chicago—one already sold. Get your order in on these cars as it is impossible to get these cars without a signed order from the buyer.

The new Buik six and four cylinders are a marvel for power and endurance.

With the line of Hudson, Nash, Buick and Saxon I solicit your orders and will try and handle your old car to the best possible advantage.

I have installed an acetylene welding outfit and am prepared to do all kinds of welding. Have first class mechanics, having just secured the services of Mr. Earl Snodgrass of Des Moines, who is thoroughly schooled on the Buick, Dodge, Reo, and Mitchell.

Have a brand new Briscoe 1918 model for sale cheap. Call and see me.

First door west of the What Cheer Savings Bank—open day and night

What Cheer Garage
F. L. Emery, Prop.

Display Ad ("To the Public") was published March 28, 1918.

A July 4 parade in which Zella Emery is driving her father's car. Mrs. Frank Emery, the dealer's wife, is the fourth woman in the car (from left), and Zella's sister Vera is the second from the right.

Frank L. Emery, What Cheer, in front of his Rambler establishment.

When IADA was formed, the attempt to keep roads in good condition was largely
the chore of horse-drawn road graders like this one crossing Main Street in
Lacona in 1918.

photo credit State Historical Society of Iowa–Des Moines

the 1920s

"Some people seem to be constitutionally opposed to hard surfaced roads. Their opposition at times has the strength of religious fanaticism. As a matter of fact, there is no justification for anyone to take the position of being blindly opposed to paving or blindly in favor of such improvements. ... Motor vehicles can be operated over pavement more cheaply than over a dirt or graveled road. ... The Iowa dirt roads are perhaps among the finest dirt roads in the country when they are sufficiently dry to be firm and stable and sufficiently wet not to be dusty. The happy condition, however, seldom prevails."

From F.R. White, chief engineer, Iowa State Highway Commission, in his address to the IAMA convention, quoted in the January, 1924, *Motor Trades Bulletin*

In 1922, the bureau changed its name to the Iowa Automotive Merchants Association (IAMA), explaining that the word "bureau … signifies a department subordinate to some organization, hence is improper as applied to our association, is misunderstood, causes confusion and lacks force."

The change reflected a quickly growing industry in Iowa. By 1922 the state had 365,000 motor vehicles. By 1923 the number climbed to 503,113. Two years later it reached 620,000. And in 1927 there were 711,951 "machines registered"—enough to transport "every man, woman and child in the state." Iowa led all states in number of cars per capita.

Despite the boom, association advertising revenues and membership suffered because "general business conditions were subnormal," and soon IAMA was operating at a deficit. As business people, auto dealers wrestled throughout the decade with financial losses in accepting used cars as trades for new ones. IAMA viewed various plans—including Appleby Plan Motomarts, NADA's plan, and the Noyes-New London plan— to end trade-in woes, but without adequate

membership or participation, the association couldn't make any effort work. The need to give used cars "value" grew, and the association sought monthly data from dealers on cars and prices so that it could compile and distribute the information to its members.

Legislation

During the 1920s, the association focused attention on securing favorable state legislation, including elimination of fees for trucks crossing into bordering states, protective measures for owners of rental batteries, funding of more hard-surface roads through a road bond program, graduated payments on licensing fees, and reduction in the transfer fee paid by licensed used car dealers.

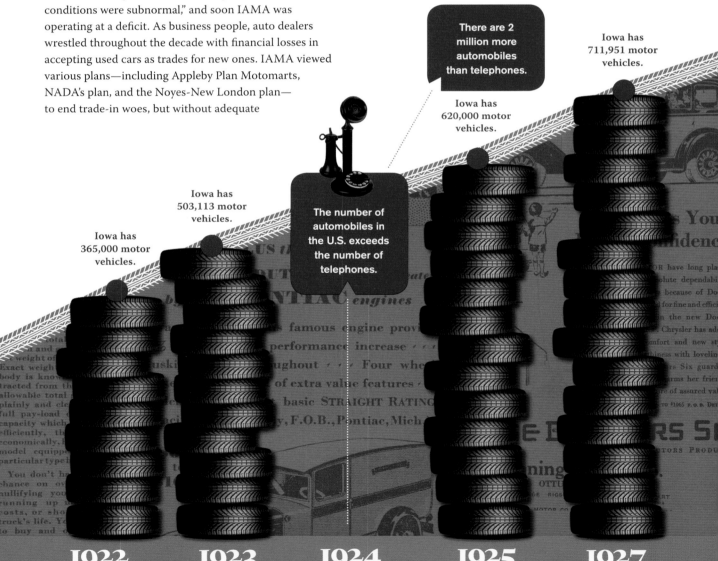

There are 2 million more automobiles than telephones.

Iowa has 711,951 motor vehicles.

Iowa has 620,000 motor vehicles.

Iowa has 503,113 motor vehicles.

The number of automobiles in the U.S. exceeds the number of telephones.

Iowa has 365,000 motor vehicles.

1922   1923   1924   1925   1927

ate Terry **LOOMIS**

Kate Terry Loomis

In all of the magazines and newsletters published by the association, only one woman–Kate Terry Loomis–was written about for her deep commitment to the motor trades, her savvy as a dealer, and the respect she earned from her peers. After the association's second convention, it was written: "Mrs. Kate Loomis, an active member of the Quigley Loomis Motor Company, Cedar Rapids, of course belongs to the Linn County Motor Trades Bureau and the IMTB. Mrs. Loomis was chairman of the entertainment committee for ladies. As her duties in that respect were not heavy, she became general counsel for all committees, and no one worked harder or was more enthusiastic. She became president of the Cedar Rapids Motomart Association when auto dealers sought to solve their used car woes through a collective merchandising center for the vehicles."

The following article appeared in the IAMA's October, 1923, *Motor Trades Bulletin*. It contains a paragraph from the *Automobile Trade Journal,* which was published monthly by Chilton Class Journal Co., Philadelphia:

Kate Terry Loomis 'Makes' Chilton's Hall of Fame

"*Readers of the* Automobile Trade Journal *no doubt noticed the following item and photograph in the September 1 issue of the magazine on the page entitled* 'We Nominate for the Automotive Hall of Fame.'

'*We nominate Kate Terry Loomis, president, Loomis Motor Company, Cedar Rapids, Iowa, because she has proved that a woman can be a far more successful automobile dealer than most men, because she is a business woman who has sacrificed no womanly qualities in attaining to success in the automotive field, because she is president of the Cedar Rapids Dealers' Association and because she has the admiration and respect of every member of the automotive trade in her home city.'*

We second that nomination. We are proud of Kate Terry Loomis. She is one of our ablest and most enthusiastic members.

(*The president of the IAMA, Dean Schooler, of Des Moines, and Harter B. Hull, a member of the association residing in Waterloo, were also nominated for the* "Hall of Fame" *several months ago.*)"

Editor's Note: No mention was made of the two gentlemen "making" Chilton's Hall of Fame.)

One month prior to the Chilton's story, the *Motor Trades Bulletin* carried the following from Mrs. Loomis regarding the work of IAMA:

What Mrs. Loomis Says

"*We quote below from Mrs. Kate Terry Loomis, of Cedar Rapids. As president and manager of the Loomis Motor Company and president of the Cedar Rapids Automobile Merchants Association, her opinion should carry weight.*

'*The extra session of the Iowa legislature, convening December 4, will entail much work upon our secretary and the directors of the association. Every member of the organization should do everything possible both with money and time to help them in securing favorable legislation and in keeping overzealous legislators from passing more unfavorable laws. Busy the trade may be, but we should not be too busy to attend to our own very necessary business, and the work that Mr. Knapp is doing for the state is just that, OUR BUSINESS.*

'*Just about the easiest thing people do these days is criticize the automobile. They forget that it is only another word for personal transportation, which has become a vital necessity. We have this transportation to sell and we want as little resistance to our efforts as possible. More co-operation among merchants engaged in the industry is the answer, more feeling that we are surely making progress, that what benefits one benefits all, and a little more willingness to do things because they help the trade, and us indirectly, will turn the trick.*

'*Let's be pushers for the big things that go with the largest industry in the world. If you are not a member of the Iowa Automotive Merchants Association, JOIN NOW. If you are a member and have not paid your dues for the next fiscal year, PAY THEM NOW and show the world that you are alive.'*"

Marshalltown's LADY DEALERS

Dealers Neil and Stockwell (no first names were given) secured the Gray contract in Marshalltown from George Peak, Des Moines distributor, and "are making a splendid success." The "girls are known around town as 'the Gray sisters'" and were referenced in the article as equal owners of Neil & Stockwell. Neil, with interests in mechanics and construction, won a sale by putting a row of shingles on a farmer's barn while he discussed a purchase with Stockwell. Stockwell, a music teacher, was known to "entertain a family with her playing and singing" and "leave with the order."
–March, 1925, *Motor Trades Bulletin*

Lester R. Glover

Used Car
MERCHANDISING

"Used cars are merchandise," wrote Harrison R. Brown in an article for the *Motor Trades Bulletin* in October, 1923. Brown was chairman of the Des Moines Dealer's Used Car Committee. "Too many of us have been handling the used car as a chattel, and we have been paying for this absurdity. If you were selling a new car which lists for $1,000, assuming that your commission is twenty percent, you would make a profit of $200. If in selling this new car you take in a used car at $500 and sell it the same day without even touching it or spending a dollar on it, many dealers would consider that this was a highly creditable and satisfactory transaction.

"The facts do not sustain this conclusion. When you accept the statement that used cars are merchandise it is impossible for you to put this transaction on your books without establishing beyond all question of argument the fact that you have done $1,500 worth of business and that you have made a $200 profit. Your commission, therefore, shrinks to thirteen and one-third percent. Six and two-thirds percent of your commission has disappeared. It is gone, and you can't bring it back, and you therefore have lost it.

"Now, if after adding your cost of conditioning to your take-in price on the used car you will add twenty-five percent profit (which is twenty percent on list price) you will add to your profit $125, and your books will therefore show that you have done $1,625 worth of business at a profit of $325. You have thus retained your full twenty percent commission and there is no other way on this green earth that you are going to do it. The argument is irrefutable."

Mr. Brown went on to comment on three facts:
1. The cost of conditioning used cars must be charged against the taken-in price.
2. Overhead must be charged against the individual used car taken in.
3. Used cars must be handled in a separate department.

"Any dealer who accepts these fundamentals before his fellow merchants but goes out and deliberately does the very opposite in his daily practices is not only dishonest with himself, his competitors and those with whom he deals," Brown wrote, "but he has no place in the business life of his community and no right to sit among his fellow men and ask that they repose confidence in him."

By 1927, the association reported that it had worked for or against some 1,200 bills since forming in 1919. In 1929, it successfully offered three bills in the legislature and found itself enjoying a good rapport with the Iowa Motor Vehicle Licensing Department and the House and Senate Motor Vehicle Committees. The association also got involved in national legislation, calling for the repeal of the federal excise tax on motor vehicles, which was enacted during the war.

The need for better roads was always on the legislative agenda because "millions of dollars are wasted in gas, oil, and depreciation to motor vehicles because of six or seven months of poor roads" and "Iowa [in 1926 was] the only state in the union in which primary roads are under control of the separate counties." The association leadership encouraged "better business methods" and adopted a code of ethics.

Services Offered

Among the services IAMA provided to its members was an audit of their railway freight bills, identifying errors and helping members receive refunds. The association

A 1929 Chevrolet outside Tuffree Chevrolet, now John Worden Garage, in Green Mountain.

also made arrangements for fire, theft, public liability, property, and workers' compensation insurance to be available to members. The monthly *Motor Trades Bulletin* provided lengthy educational write-ups from convention speakers (as convention attendance was dropping), news of scams and charlatans making their way around the state, legislative accomplishments, and advertising to support the publication. Some 52,000 copies were sent in 1928, an average of 4,333 per month. The call for non-members—and delinquent members—to "pay their way" was ongoing in the publication.

Changes in Membership

By 1924 membership in IAMA dropped to 585 and the association's deficit approached $3,000. Efforts continued to secure membership from the dealers who received the benefits, but most failed to join. "The newcomers in our ranks are not aware that the state association made possible the lowered price of dealers' plates, the used-car dealers' licenses, the listing privilege and many other advantages they now enjoy," wrote editor A.J. Knapp in May, 1925. "The passage of the battery bill the past winter was a real achievement, particularly in view of the fact that so many other states refused to enact it."

Knapp left in August of 1925 for an opportunity in Florida, and T.W. Le Quatte took the position. But Knapp returned nine months later and assumed the secretary-manager spot again. In 1925, the auto industry nationwide reached first place in the commodity market, passing both the steel and packing industries. "Much as I dislike to admit it," wrote Knapp in August, 1926, "the fact remains that there are too many licensed dealers who have no business ability, and that is just where, in my opinion, the manufacturer can and should help the situation." Knapp left the association again in May of 1927, and Walter Ferrell took over staff leadership in June.

"Our industry has been much like a bull pup, big and awkward, with a ravenous appetite and a framework covered by a skin large enough for a full-grown dog. Full of the devil, strong but with no conception of its strength, it has taken the kicks, cuffs and knocks with the grace of a well bred and well fed pup and seldom has retaliated. ... While the industry has been growing, realizing its strength and exerting it in some ways, it has failed utterly to sense the need for applying its strength in other equally important directions. I refer particularly to the lack of unity in finding remedies and applying them to correct the bad practices within our business, and to prevent the further encroachment of elements from the outside."
—Andy Knapp, IAMA secretary-manager,
January, 1925, *Motor Trades Bulletin*

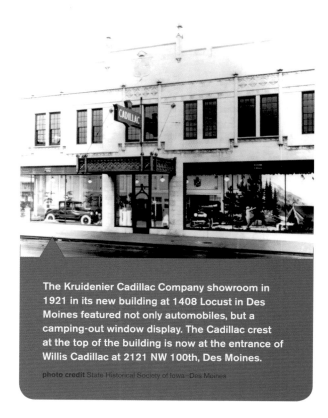

The Kruidenier Cadillac Company showroom in 1921 in its new building at 1408 Locust in Des Moines featured not only automobiles, but a camping-out window display. The Cadillac crest at the top of the building is now at the entrance of Willis Cadillac at 2121 NW 100th, Des Moines.

photo credit State Historical Society of Iowa–Des Moines

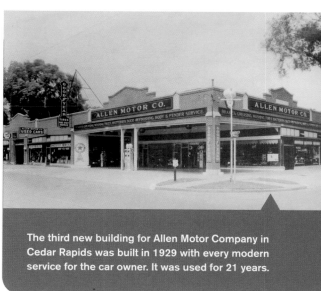

The third new building for Allen Motor Company in Cedar Rapids was built in 1929 with every modern service for the car owner. It was used for 21 years.

Industry Relationships

According to the group's magazine, relationships between dealers and the factories were visibly strained by the middle of the decade over such topics as "lack of understanding of the dealer's needs and opportunities … longer dealer contracts … discounts … improvement in methods of merchandising and distributing parts." Wrestling with the issue of open territory vis-à-vis closed territory, in July of 1924, Knapp wrote, "I believe territorial lines must be established, and in so doing great care must be given to the natural trend of the buying public toward specific trading centers. Competition between different lines is sufficient, indeed, to stimulate dealers to put forth every effort; but when competition between men selling the same make of car is added, the result spells two things, profits for the factory and losses for the dealer."

In July of that year Knapp wrote, "Conditions in this industry aren't good, and they never will be until the merchandising methods from factory to consumer are revised. No industry can prosper unless the distributor and dealer prosper along with the manufacturer."

Iowa dealers reported that in 1928 they sold 87,711 automobiles and made money; in 1929, they sold 108,340 autos and made no money. Some 80 percent were ready to sell their businesses for less than inventory value. IAMA advised its frustrated dealers not to "get panicky" and warned them that "discussing dealer or distributor problems with the public" was "suicide." By December of 1929, car dealers were calling for manufacturers to cut production because output was exceeding replacement demand, and businesses were feeling the impact of "the crash of stocks in the east."

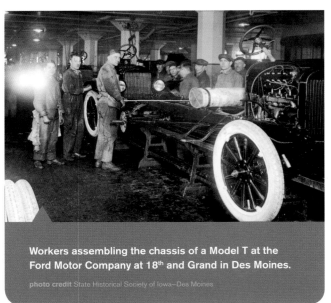

Workers assembling the chassis of a Model T at the Ford Motor Company at 18th and Grand in Des Moines.

photo credit State Historical Society of Iowa–Des Moines

Family Dealership

Throughout IADA's history, dealerships have been passed from one generation to the next, primarily from fathers to sons. Three generations of the Braga family ran new automobile dealerships from 1923 to 2004.

1923

I.W. (Irving) Braga purchased East Side Auto at 120 East Rocksylvania in Iowa Falls and simply named it I.W. Braga. He sold Dodge cars and trucks the first year and added the Hupmobile, Star, Garant, and Studebaker a year later. Pontiac, Dodge and Plymouth also were among the cars sold over the years.

1942

The business moved to the corner of Oak and Estes.

1924

I.W. Braga (at right) stands with an unknown customer in the 1920s as the bricks adorned with "East Side Auto Company" begin to fade.

LASTS GENERATIONS

1951
Pictured in 1951 at the showing of 1952 cars are I.W. Braga (second from left) and his sons Stanley, Marvin and DeVere.

1948
Three of Braga's four sons—DeVere, Marvin, and Stanley—were partners in I.W. Braga & Sons.

1957
I.W. died.

1962
Marvin sold out to his brothers. They continued to sell new vehicles at the same location until 1989. Marvin bought Vaughn Manning Rambler and Imports and renamed it Braga Motor Company.

1970s
Marvin added the Jeep franchise, a new garage, and his two sons, Brad and Mark, to the business. Over the years the company held Rambler, Chrysler, and Plymouth franchises.

1989
I.W. Braga & Sons ceases sale of new vehicles in Iowa Falls.

2004
Braga Motor Company sold in Marshalltown.

2007
The Iowa Falls location is a used-car dealership run by DeVere's son, Ron.

1948
In 1948, as a second generation of Bragas joined their father, a new showroom was built onto an existing service station at 320 Oak Street in Iowa Falls (U.S. highways 65 and 20).

UYER'S · GUIDE

1934 EDITION

A sequel to *"The Proving Ground of Public Opinion"* —reflecting the views of 211,000 motorists responding to General Motors consumer research surveys.

problem since 1930, conducting tests and making studies and computations of such high-sounding things as *"periodicity", "oscillation", "harmonics"* and *"moment of inertia."*

If you could see all the sketches, diagrams and charts that were worked out incident to the preliminary researches you might easily *MISTAKE THEM FOR DR. EINSTEIN'S ORIGINAL WORKING PAPERS!*

Now, of course no one but an engineer would be able to understand the mathematics of the thing—but you don't have to understand the engineering theories in order to appreciate what it means

these new cars behave when encountering irregularities in the road.

With the wheels held in alignment *independently of the springs,* we can make the springs just as soft as we want them. And with the new coil spring construction it's possible to get a *LONGER SPRING TRAVEL* than with the old-style construction.

The car naturally rides smoother *UNDER ALL CONDITIONS* because of the softer springs and the longer spring action. When you strike a ridge in the road—such as a car track, a railroad crossing, a culvert—the softer

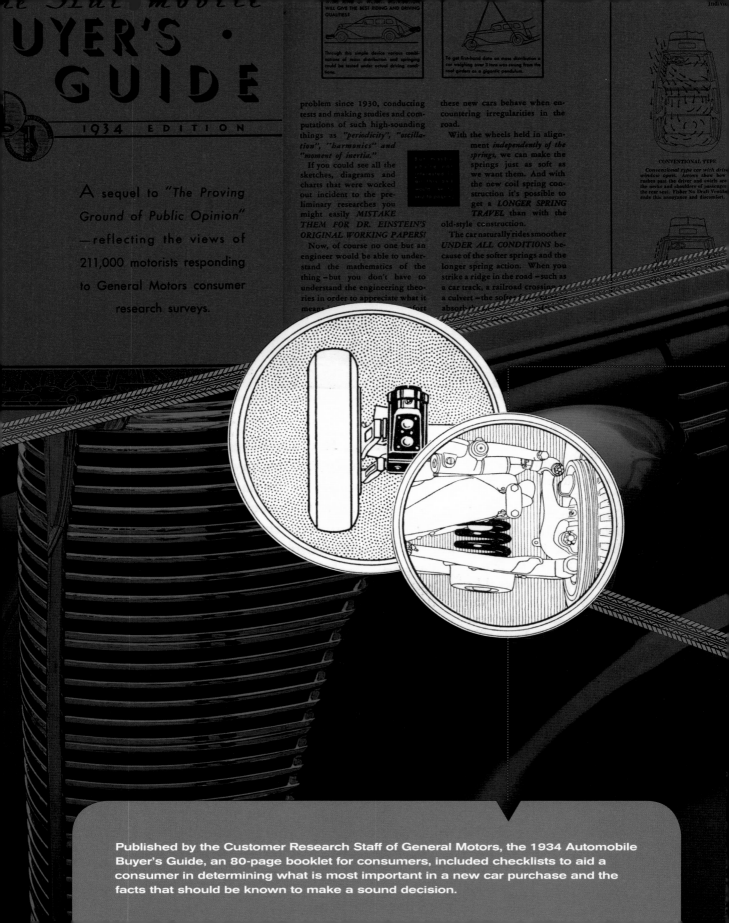

Published by the Customer Research Staff of General Motors, the 1934 Automobile Buyer's Guide, an 80-page booklet for consumers, included checklists to aid a consumer in determining what is most important in a new car purchase and the facts that should be known to make a sound decision.

"During the '30s the Depression, with all the banks closing, made selling cars difficult even with the low prices we sometimes had to offer. Financing was hard to get, and cash downpayments on automobiles were very scarce. We sold many automobiles to people who could make the small monthly payments necessary to pay out the contract in not over 12 months of trading for their wives' diamond rings. There was no market for diamonds at jewelry store prices, but we were able to offer ours at low prices and our market was to young men who had jobs and a girl who wanted a diamond. For several years we created our own diamond market. Also, we traded for guns as down payments on cars, mostly in the spring and selling in the fall and winter when the hunting season was open. Our business was selling automobiles and this only helped make this possible in those difficult times."

–**Lester R. Glover,** Wapello County, who began his 50 years as an automobile dealer in 1919 (written in 1969)

Early in the decade IAMA stayed optimistic in its communication with members, calling for them to "dig in, work harder, overcome the lack of desire to buy and the fear of spending." Members were told: "Business depressions are periodic. They seem to strike about every ten years. They have occurred with fair regularity for some time, but each time the affected depression is less. Those who compare present conditions with those that prevailed in 1921, and base them on facts, will find that the present depression is comparatively light as compared with that of 1921."

At the same time, dealers were told to look for new ways to make money. C.A. Vane, general manager of NADA wrote, "Profits are no longer in the delivery of new vehicles but in the maintenance and repair of old ones." Dealers sought profit wherever they could find it, and by the end of 1931, shotgun shells were among the 20 best-selling lines of merchandise at the average garage. The association urged members to become Authorized Safety Service Stations to profit from inspection program income.

Membership and Income Instability

Throughout the '30s, membership numbers fluctuated significantly, and the association struggled to stay solvent. In 1931 at IAMA's annual meeting and convention, secretary-manager Walter Ferrell reported that membership had increased from 890 to 1,092, but 236 were delinquent in dues. The association was debt-free and for the first time had members in every Iowa county.

By 1932, 462 of 1,025 members were delinquent. IAMA temporarily eliminated its telephone, had no field representative, and office help worked only three days per week. That year Ferrell took a salary as low as $50 a month—whatever was left at month's end. Members were warned that by fall, "There is extreme danger of not having the association to stand on guard and protect the industry as it has in the past. It is certain that the office will have to close November 1, 1932 unless members send in at least a portion of their delinquent dues between now and then." October's office rent was $25, wages were $68.25, and office supplies were 60 cents.

In March, 1933, there were 74 members in good standing—a stark contrast to the 856 who paid just two years earlier—although there were believed to be 4,055 automotive merchants in Iowa. Alfred A. Bruesewitz, owner of Bruesewitz Chevrolet, sold just two cars in all of 1933. "But we got by," he recalled. A dues reduction in 1934 forced the association to survive on less than $4,000 for the year.

The impact of the Depression can be seen by the reduction in the size of the shop staff at Kruidenier Cadillac between 1930 (top photo) and 1931 (bottom photo).

"The present depression has now been with us about a year and the one thing that is troubling the minds of most interested is as to the length of the low period. It is generally conceded, however, that the bottom has at least been reached and that any change in the immediate future will be for the better."
—June, 1931, *Motor Trades Bulletin*

By September, 1935, IAMA was in debt, and Ferrell continued to take home what dollars were left over when monthly bills were paid. He reported that only 24 of the state's 1,334 non-dealer garages were association members, so IAMA was carrying the non-dealer unit at a financial loss. "It may or may not be the proper time to submit to the pressure of NADA, manufacturers, and a large number of dealers and turn the association into a 'dealer organization' as many other states have successfully done," he said.

In March, 1936, amended bylaws changed the association name to the Iowa Automobile Dealers Association (IADA) and called for the election of a director from each county. Returning to a dues schedule of $50, $25 or $15 for various levels of annual sales helped the association recover momentarily, but leaders said IADA's future success depended "almost wholly upon a membership of 1,000." Membership in good standing was 246 from 71 counties at

the time, and troubles continued. In 1937 membership was 152, and 47 counties were not identified with IADA. Total receipts were $13,688. In October, 1939, Ferrell, without giving a number, wrote, "membership has decreased to a new and almost disgraceful low."

Throughout the '30s, IADA's leadership never quit requesting dues, citing continued dealer savings, legislative successes, and the merits of trade associations. The *Bulletin* frequently contained quotes gathered from other trade associations, such as this by O.H. Cheney, a prominent New York banker, in a speech to the Sheet Metal Ware Association convention: "Trade association membership is a measure of character because it shows the member's ability to get along with others. Trade association membership is a measure of intelligence of the member's business methods because he is trying to eliminate competitive waste and to use cooperation as an economical promotion weapon."

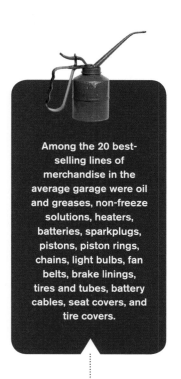

Among the 20 best-selling lines of merchandise in the average garage were oil and greases, non-freeze solutions, heaters, batteries, sparkplugs, pistons, piston rings, chains, light bulbs, fan belts, brake linings, tires and tubes, battery cables, seat covers, and tire covers.

MARCH
For the first time, IAMA has members in every county of the state.

Membership increases from 890 to 1,092, but 236 are delinquent in dues.

JANUARY
One of ten people who are gainfully employed in the United States helped to make, sell, and service cars.

462 of 1,025 members are delinquent.

MARCH
74 members in good standing

Alfred A. Bruesewitz, owner of Bruesewitz Chevrolet, sells just two cars in all of 1933.

Return to a dues schedule of $50, $25 or $15 for various levels of annual sales.

Membership is 152, and 47 counties are not identified with IADA.

OCTOBER
Ferrell, without giving a number, wrote, "membership has decreased to a new and almost disgraceful low."

Iowa has 5,090 miles of paved highway, placing it sixth in the United States and first among all states west of the Mississippi in total miles of paving.

1931   1932   1933   1936   1937   1939

National Scene: Taxation

At the beginning of 1932, dealers felt business was turning around, and that a massive advertising and sales effort would prompt consumers to replace one million motor vehicles already used "beyond the limit of safe and economic service." But a huge deficit in the U.S. Treasury brought a recommendation that "a further burden of taxation shall be imposed upon the motor vehicle industry by an excise tax of 5 percent on automobiles, 3 percent on trucks and 2.5 percent on motor vehicle parts, tires and accessories."

In April, Ferrell wrote, "The Treasury continues to recommend excise taxes and now proposes a federal levy of 1 cent per gallon in addition to the present state levy of 3 cents per gallon on gasoline." Effective June 20, a national excise tax was added to passenger motor vehicles (3 percent), trucks (2 percent), accessories and parts (2 percent), and 1 cent per gallon of gasoline, 4 cents per gallon on lubricating oil, 2.5 cents per pound on motor vehicle tires and 4 cents per pound on inner tubes.

Trouble in Manufacturer-Dealer Relations

Before mid-1932, NADA general manager C.A.Vane began preaching about "a grossly unjust relationship existing between manufacturers and dealers since its onset." He wrote the following: "Between 1920 and 1929, the eighteen principal American manufacturers made total net profits equal to the total value of all gold mined in this country in 113 years. … Since 1929 we, in common with all lines of business, have had a hard time. Dealers and manufacturers have had two years in which to straighten up affairs, but so far as I have been able to see, the sole suggestion emanating from Detroit and like centers of production for dealer help is 'Get more car sales. Volume means profit.' Well, that is what they told us in 1922 after the bottom fell out in 1921. That's what they told us in 1928 after the sales recession of 1927. That's what they're telling us in 1932, after the crash of 1929 in which the industry made 5,625,000 motor vehicles, an all-time record for production and for subsequent washout of dealer capital. Three times we fell for the suggestion. Are we going to swallow the bait the fourth time?"

In May, 1933, association leaders spoke out: "We believe the time is at hand when the federal government will soon exercise some supervision over factory production, based upon a study of the probable automobile market

Words to eight songs were listed in the Chevrolet Song Sheet from the 1932 meeting for dealers and salesmen. This "Features Song" was sung to the tune of "East Side, West Side."

North—South—East—West,
Ev-ery-where you go,
Roads are filled with speed-ing cars—
They're wear-ing out we know.
Own-ers must re-place them
With trans-por-ta-tion that's new.
They're all worn out
And can't make the grade
In Nine-teen Thir-ty Two.

Pros-pects, pros-pects—
Now let's get their "Dough."
Talk to them about Synro-Mesh ,
More power, speed and "go."
Smart, new Fish-er bodies,
Simple Free Wheeling that's new,
So Chev-ro-let will lead all the world
In Nine-teen Thir-ty Two.

in any given year. Supervision will be of great benefit to automobile dealers who have been continually overloaded by their factories and thus forced to give over allowances on used cars in order to move their stock."

In June, 1933, auto dealers began putting their hopes in the National Industrial Recovery Act (NIRA), which focused on "regulatory measures governing business for greater public benefit." The act gave industry the power to "regulate its own affairs and places the responsibility for doing it squarely upon its own shoulders." Considered "extremely revolutionary," the act gave trade associations a major role. IAMA believed that "within 90 days automotive merchants in Iowa will be begging us to accept their dues and allow them membership in the association."

The association immediately went to work on a suggested Automotive Industry Code for Iowa, a code for fair competition "prepared for the purpose of bringing into harmonious association all corporations, partnerships and individuals now or hereafter engaged in and connected with the automotive industry in the state of Iowa and for the further purpose of stabilizing and increasing employment and business within the industry to accomplish the objects set forth in the NIRA." It addressed such areas as fair and reasonable working hours, compensation for employees, fair and reasonable profit, trade practices detrimental to the automotive industry and individuals, and fair and reasonable values to the consumer.

The Automotive Industry Code for Iowa was submitted to NADA, the entity charged with directing the nation's automotive code, in hopes that Iowa's thoughtful contribution would help NADA in developing its document. The final Code for the Motor Vehicle Retailing Trade was approved by President Franklin Roosevelt and became effective October 3, 1933. It was believed that all transactions of all businesses throughout the U.S. would soon be code-dominated. In Iowa, a state advisory committee was set up by IAMA to address code violations for the automobile industry.

To control the fair trade-in of used cars, the NADA Used Car Official Guide—the only manual of values authorized by the Code—was to be used. Based on dealer reporting, it would devise a system to determine market values. But in June, 1935, the U.S. Supreme Court ruled that Congress exceeded its authority in permitting President Roosevelt to promulgate codes and declared all NIRA codes invalid. Ferrell wrote, "The decision removed the last vestige of restraint. Hereafter whatever is done to regulate chiseling price-cutters must be done by and through majority dealers

Ryal Miller (left) is pictured with an unknown gentlemen in front of Miller's Sioux City dealership, Ryal Miller Chevrolet Company, in the 1930s. The dealership would become Ryal Miller-Kidder, Miller-Kidder Co., Kidder-Knoepfler, and then Knoepfler Chevrolet Company. Miller was IADA president in 1931.

working together in local, state and national associations. Dealers hoping to survive should apply sane business judgment and follow the principles laid down in the Motor Vehicle Code of Fair Competition."

With the loss of the codes, dealers nationwide sought new ways to change their relationships with factories, which they considered coercive. On May 28, 1937, Congressman Gardner Withrow of Wisconsin introduced a joint resolution to the 75th Congress, directing the Federal Trade Commission to investigate the policies employed by manufacturers in factory-dealer relationships. Early in 1938, IADA's Walter Ferrell testified in Washington, D.C., keeping his remarks focused on coercion—primarily contracts that dealers could not cancel, problems with open territories, dealers being forced to take cars they didn't want, prepaid freight bills and "undercapitalized, unfit, and insolvent" persons who received factory contracts to sell cars to family members and friends.

In September, 1938, Ferrell wrote, "The very fact that manufacturers are against [the resolution] is plenty of reason for retail dealers to be for it." The lengthy FTC findings, reported in August, 1939, stated that "inequities exist in the

"There are 26 million automobile owners in the U.S. Only 9 million of them have ever purchased and owned new cars. By this it is clear that the used car business has helped rather than hindered retail dealers. It is not the used car but what dealers have done with used cars that has made trade-ins an evil."
—November, 1937, *Iowa Automobile Dealers Bulletin*

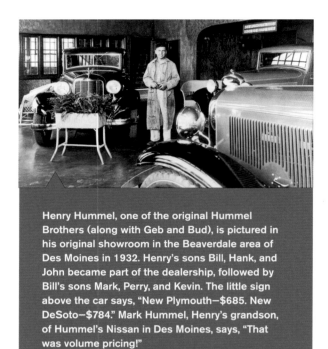

Henry Hummel, one of the original Hummel Brothers (along with Geb and Bud), is pictured in his original showroom in the Beaverdale area of Des Moines in 1932. Henry's sons Bill, Hank, and John became part of the dealership, followed by Bill's sons Mark, Perry, and Kevin. The little sign above the car says, "New Plymouth—$685. New DeSoto—$784." Mark Hummel, Henry's grandson, of Hummel's Nissan in Des Moines, says, "That was volume pricing!"

"If the railroads and the street cars were killing as many people as automobiles none of us would ride on them. … We are attempting to educate the people to influence legislators to provide a law requiring compulsory, periodical inspection of the safety equipment on motor vehicles. … A majority of the 900,000 motor vehicles operated in Iowa need mechanical attention and adjustment and we believe the owners will cooperate if the matter is urgently called to their attention."
—December, 1931, *Iowa Automotive Merchants Bulletin*

terms of dealer agreements, and in certain manufacturers' treatment of some dealers, calling for remedial action." It was recommended that "present unfair practices be abated," and the findings cited a number of areas to be addressed. Three months later at its San Francisco convention, NADA unveiled a five-point franchise contract that would attempt to govern manufacturer-dealer relations.

State Legislative Action

Throughout this difficult decade, the association's approach to each state legislative session entailed "supporting all regulatory measures for regulation and control of motor vehicles and opposing tax measures designed and offered to increase the daily cost of operations." At least 20 percent of the bills introduced during a session—typically 1,000+ but as low as 689 in 1934—impacted the automotive industry. Because regulation of the young automotive industry was an evolving task, the IADA sought amendments to sections of Iowa's newer laws throughout the 1930s.

With gasoline taxes amounting to 15 to 20 percent of the cost of the product, the association successfully held off additional state increases. They fought for a Mechanic's Lien Law, a measure that would have established "who is and who is not a motor vehicle dealer."

They also advocated paving for Iowa's primary roads and the graveling of secondary roads leading to them, and for a uniformed state traffic patrol supervised by the Motor Vehicle Licensing Department. The association gave itself credit for practically stopping fraudulent new car registrations in Iowa.

IADA successfully pushed for legislation that placed used motor vehicles on an unlicensed dealer (UD) list for reduced dealer fees, restored license fee refund rights, secured the Iowa Fair Trade Practices Law to eliminate fraudulent advertising, and lowered licensing fees beginning with the fourth registration of passenger cars.

The association helped defeat a "port of entry law" and a "ton-mile tax on motor trucks" in 1935 and fought such "silly" bills as one to require county treasurers to withhold the licensing of vehicles until the owners paid their old-age pension tax.

A two percent state retail sales tax was enacted to run from April 1, 1934, to April 1, 1937, to replenish Iowa's depleted treasury. While the association was not opposed to the tax—"dealers want to pay their fair share"—they did object to its application on receipts from the exchange and subsequent sale of used motor vehicles. They fought successfully to have that portion of the rule eliminated. It was in force for only six weeks, but clarification of the retail sales law as it related to the automobile industry continued for some time.

IADA leaders called 1937 "the most important legislative session to date" and presented an association bill they called the Dealer License Law. It did everything from license and regulate persons engaged in the automotive business to prescribe penalties for non-compliance with the Dealer License Law. It was enacted that year, along with a uniform standard motor vehicle law and legislation that made the retail sales tax on motor vehicles an excise tax collected at the time of licensing by county treasurers.

In 1938, IADA worked with the Motor Vehicle Department to bring a quick end to the dumping of Eastern state surpluses of used cars into Iowa, and then

In 1930, Des Moines brothers Ralph and Rolland Davis set a world record for "non-stop auto endurance." Described as "boys with an ambition to do something different," they drove a Model A Ford non-stop—meaning day and night—for 113 days and 47,138.3 miles in a run at the record. They were sponsored by Capitol Motors, Inc., Des Moines Ford dealers.

According to a newsletter account of their non-stop motoring efforts, "the boys encountered thrills a plenty to balance the unexpected grief and some unpleasant experiences." Their adventure began when Parker Crouch, Des Moines mayor, started the pair in front of the Register and Tribune building at 7 p.m. on August 1. They were officially stopped at 10:46 a.m. on November 23 by John Hammill, Iowa's governor, in front of the State Capitol building.

"The previous record recognized by the American Automobile Association, was established by a Marmon car and the total mileage was 13,457.5. The new record by the Davis brothers is nearly three times greater. The car, when stopped, was in excellent mechanical condition and could have gone on for a much greater mileage except for inconveniences experienced by the boys due to early cold weather."

The car provided by Capitol Motors was a "Model A panel job Ford from their regular stock." Gas and oil were furnished by Texaco Oil Co., and tires were supplied by Kelly-Springfield Tire Co. "Tire changes were made with the aid of a rolling dolly under the axles which enabled one of the boys to change the tire as the car moved slowly along its way. This particular wheel changing feature was demonstrated before the State Fair visitors in August during the first 30 days of the run."

The boys' parents moved to Ankeny from their residence on East 13th Street in Des Moines "to be near the boys at all times necessary and to provide them with a headquarters that would be away from the busy Des Moines streets. Both boys agreed that their mother is entitled to the most credit for her encouragement, riding miles with them "regardless of the weather," providing healthy food and "looking after their needs," the newsletter said.

"During the first half of the run the boys lived entirely within the walls of the panel body car. They discontinued this when they found they were not obtaining sufficient exercise, and from that time on to keep in fit condition they exercised alternately by trotting along the side of the car."

Keeping the car moving at all times proved interesting. When caught between two freight trains in Waterloo, the boys found a third parallel railroad track and drove down it until they found the next crossing. The Davis brothers had their "biggest thrill" near Lake Mills when "a bandit car drew across the road ahead of them." Men at either end of the car had "pistols in their hands." The brothers were nearing the old world record, so Ralph, 20, "stepped on the gas and Rolland, 25, stood on the running board pointing to the printed signs on the car" (which spelled out the fact they were driving a world endurance car). They managed to speed around the "bandit car" without going in the ditch or being forced to stop.

West of Ames one day the brothers encountered a disgruntled motorist—"evidently disgusted with having met and passed the endurance car on the road so often"—who attempted to drive in front of them and stop their vehicle. Their car was forced into a ditch, but the boys recovered and kept the Ford moving.

The pair hoped to make some money from the successful event, pay off the mortgage on their family's home, and go into business for themselves. The article stated that a "tour of the United States for the purpose of advertising Iowa and her good roads is already under preparation. Iowa can well afford to contribute to such an advertising campaign which will make it possible for the boys to cash in on their efforts."

–December, 1930, *Iowa Automotive Merchants Bulletin*

Dealers were always looking for ways to show their community spirit and promote their businesses. Schukei Chevrolet, Waterloo, supported athletic teams.

addressed problems with licensing reciprocity across state lines with Illinois dealers. In 1939, the Farm To Market Road Plan passed to "give Iowa a splendid secondary system without increasing gas tax or increased cost to motor vehicle users."

Safety Concerns Continue

The association, which had ongoing concerns about vehicle safety, asked the 1931 legislature to enact a law for periodic inspections and urged members to be part of inspection programs. A Play Safe campaign in 1932 inspected 12,000 vehicles in its first two weeks, keeping 300 official inspection service stations busy. In 1934 IADA urged dealers to contact their city governments to make September "Motor Safety Month." In 1938, IADA worked with the Iowa Safety Councils on the "Save 100 Lives" campaign that promoted 12 safe driving rules and safety courses taught at Iowa State College in Ames.

Leo McEleney

The growing number of aging cars on the road troubled IADA. In March, 1939, Leo McEleney of Clinton—"a man of splendid character anxious for the welfare of the dealer body"—produced a Uniform Junk Car Plan. With an estimated "five million ten-year-old, obsolete and mechanically unsafe cars on our highways," Iowa dealers were asked to test the plan. The group's publication contained no further mention of the plan.

By the 1930s dealers were already being recognized for their years of involvement in the automotive industry, as illustrated by the photo of a "Chevrolet Old Timers Banquet," where attendees were seated based on years in business.

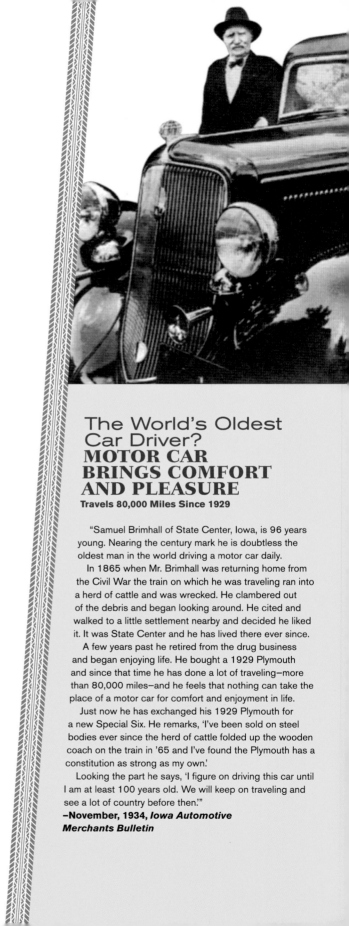

The World's Oldest Car Driver?
MOTOR CAR BRINGS COMFORT AND PLEASURE
Travels 80,000 Miles Since 1929

"Samuel Brimhall of State Center, Iowa, is 96 years young. Nearing the century mark he is doubtless the oldest man in the world driving a motor car daily.

In 1865 when Mr. Brimhall was returning home from the Civil War the train on which he was traveling ran into a herd of cattle and was wrecked. He clambered out of the debris and began looking around. He cited and walked to a little settlement nearby and decided he liked it. It was State Center and he has lived there ever since.

A few years past he retired from the drug business and began enjoying life. He bought a 1929 Plymouth and since that time he has done a lot of traveling—more than 80,000 miles—and he feels that nothing can take the place of a motor car for comfort and enjoyment in life.

Just now he has exchanged his 1929 Plymouth for a new Special Six. He remarks, 'I've been sold on steel bodies ever since the herd of cattle folded up the wooden coach on the train in '65 and I've found the Plymouth has a constitution as strong as my own.'

Looking the part he says, 'I figure on driving this car until I am at least 100 years old. We will keep on traveling and see a lot of country before then.'"
–November, 1934, *Iowa Automotive Merchants Bulletin*

7 Horses Can Pull A Load That 6 Can't Budge
That's Why We Have Trade Associations

Iowa Automobile Dealers Bulletin

Official Publication Of The

Iowa Automobile Dealers Association

A Non-profit Service Organization Representing the Automotive Industry
Office Headquarters — 1011 Locust Street — Des Moines

Association Officers and Executive Committee

President	C. A. Morris	Morris Motor Car Company	Waterloo
Vice President	R. H. Allen	Allen Motor Company	Cedar Rapids
Past President	Floyd E. Hughes	Hughes Motor Company	Council Bluffs
Treasurer	A. B. Chambers	Chambers Motor Company	Des Moines
Secretary	Walter Ferrell	Association Headquarters	Des Moines
Attorney	Tom B. Roberts	Valley National Bank Bldg.	Des Moines

Volume XVII	JUNE 1936 OFFICIAL BULLETIN	Number 11

1935 USED CAR LOSSES COST AVERAGE DEALER $50.00 PER NEW CAR SOLD

This was Potential Net Profit

THROWN AWAY...WASTED

HOW ABOUT 1936?

You can control your Used Car operations
You can reduce your daily losses . . . .
By using the N. A. D. A. Used Car Guide.

N.A.D.A. USED CAR GUIDE

This is an industry service . . . built by dealers for dealers and supplied at cost . . . Based on actual dealer used car selling experience, it tells you the market value of used cars in

Readers of the association's publications were continually reminded that the industry load is lightened when more dealers join together to work through membership in IADA and NADA. The message utilizing the work horse illustration was used frequently in the 1930s.

The paving of a road with concrete was enough to draw a crowd in July, 1941, at the junction of highways 30 and 169 in Ogden.

the 1940s

"Then the war came along and if ever an industry was given consideration by the public, we were given it then—the majority of the people marveling at our ability to stay in business and service the cars and trucks that were so sadly needed in the War effort. During the past year or year and one half we have lost a lot of this fine public support due to the fact that a few have taken advantage of the situation. These few have soured many because of the tactics used in used car and new car transactions and methods of delivery. The challenge that we have before us and within our jurisdiction is how are we going to recapture and hold this confidence so that the public will consider us as fair, equitable and honest retailers."

–G. O. Fletcher, IADA president, May, 1947, *Iowa Automobile Dealers Bulletin*

At the beginning of the decade, Iowa's primary road system of 9,570 miles carried 2.5 billion vehicle-miles per year. IADA believed there were 1,858 automobile dealers in the state, but membership in the association was "abnormally low," with more than 500 dealers delinquent in their dues.

Developing better relationships between dealers and manufacturers was a priority, but IADA, like organizations in other states, did not support "legislation designed to secure federal supervision of manufacturer-dealer franchises with a view toward federal control of manufacturer-dealer relations." Despite these concerns, the IADA's focus soon changed, as world events left Iowa dealers without new cars to sell.

Industry Converts for Defense Production

In October, 1941, President Roosevelt called a special session of Congress to repeal the law against selling munitions to countries at war. American manufacturers began receiving orders from the British and French governments for aircraft and munitions. As resources were earmarked for defense production, automobile dealers anticipated lower production of 1942 vehicles.

The bombing of Pearl Harbor on December 7, 1941, changed what had once looked like a promising decade for dealers. During World War II, they tried to keep their businesses open amid ever-changing regulations that restricted every aspect of their operations: what they had to sell, when they could sell it, who they could sell it to, how inventory had to be stored, and what prices they could charge for new and used vehicles and repair services.

Rationing Hits

The order to ration rubber came on December 27, 1941. A few days later, even bigger news arrived. On January 1, 1942, IADA President Ben Sanders wrote the membership: "Little did we expect on New Year's Eve when we were ushering out 1941 that on the first day of the new year there would be a ban on the sale of new cars by the freezing of all new cars in dealers' hands. … We must keep in mind the main purpose causing this curtailment and realize now that we are out to win this war." The freeze didn't apply just to 1942 vehicles; it extended to 1941 models that had been driven less than 1,000 miles.

NADA President Harry Sommers wrote, "The nation has embarked on a program of restriction and sacrifices to end the war by complete mobilization for victory rather than face the danger of defeat in a long war while business goes on as usual. Automobile dealers are making greater sacrifices in this emergency because they belong to an industry that the people of America look to in their hopes of winning the war. It is the auto industry that has given up its own business to produce the vital weapons of war."

MAY
The average worker drew a weekly paycheck of $32.90 during the first six months of 1940.

Ninety-two percent of the new cars and 60 percent of the used cars sold in 1940 involved the trade-in of other used cars. Only 6 percent of such used cars were junked.

JULY
About one-fourth of automobile workers had ten or more years experience in the industry.

It took 204 used-car deals to complete one new-car deal in the U.S.

DECEMBER
The distance for which gasoline could be used to deliver a newly purchased new or used car was set at a maximum of 200 miles.

DECEMBER
2.59 million families nationwide had "purchasing an automobile" at the top of the list of things they intended to buy after the war.

SEPTEMBER
129 used cars were sold in Blackhawk County between August 1 and 11. Of those, 20 were sold by dealers and 109 by individuals.

JULY
According to records kept by rural mail carriers on car operating costs, the cost per mile was 7.8 cents for earth roads, 4.5 cents for gravel roads, and 3.8 cents for paved roads.

QUALITY TAKES THE SPOTLIGHT

Will Not Loan On Or Purchase Vehicles Produced After May 11, 1942

The Board of Directors of RFC believes that the Murray-Patman Act was designed to relieve distress among automobile dealers with reference to their

33 Million Cars and Trucks Still Operating

AUTOMOTIVE NEWS — just a few less than 2,000,000 passenger cars and trucks disappeared from the streets and highways of the United States during 1942, according to a compilation made from official reports to the National Automobile Dealers Association. 18% of these cars was lost in

Amendment 6 to M Amendment 6 to MPR effective May 9, 1945 and designed to require that: "It shall be a viola regulation for any per to sell a used car by in any publication un stated in the advert price, and a notice co words "Within OPA cei words which express meaning."

A number of other min

1940   1941   1942   1943   1944   1945

50 years earlier, cars first appeared on Detroit streets. On Thanksgiving Day, 1895, Chicago was the scene of America's first automobile road race. In its first 50 years, the auto industry produced $63 billion worth of motor vehicles and more than $30 billion worth of weapons for use in two world wars.

Loved His Jeep
IN EUROPE

M.C. "Mel" White, an Oldsmobile dealer in Harlan, was "one of the boys who spent three years with the Army in Europe. Mrs. White kept the business alive while Mel did the fighting. When the war was over, he says he asked permission to bring his jeep back to the United States, and General Eisenhower granted his request because he (Mel) had kept the same jeep through every campaign he was in. The jeep was issued to him in England with seven miles on the odometer. He drove it through England, Wales, Scotland, France, Luxembourg, Belgium, Holland, Germany, Denmark, Italy, and finally the United States. It is now doing duty in his business at Harlan, and has 54,000 miles on it. Mr. White says his jeep was in 12 battles, and has five campaign stars, one tire being shot away at St. Lo. Mr. White says he and his jeep carried both Ernie Pyle and Ernest Hemmingway to the front for news and photographs."
–July, 1946, *Iowa Automobile Dealers Bulletin*

NOTE: Mel White died in 1976 (his Olds-Cadillac dealership was sold several years before his death), and his jeep was later put on display by the local historical society. The jeep was eventually sold to current Omaha resident Bruce Nelsen, who first saw the vehicle at age 14 while watching a parade in Harlan with his grandfather. Nelsen purchased the jeep in 1985. With the aid of a World War II veteran—a mechanic—in Texas, the jeep was again put in running order. A member of the Military Vehicle Collectors' Club, Nelsen has shared the jeep's story with everyone from his neighbor kids in Houston (who received rides around the block) to history buffs attending auto shows and parades. Today, the jeep typically appears in Veterans Day parades. Nelsen has looked into placing the jeep in The National World War II Museum in New Orleans.

JULY
Only eight states had more hard-surfaced roads than Iowa, which ranked fourth in number of miles of concrete roads.

AUGUST
One out of seven persons employed in the U.S. worked for the auto industry.

OCTOBER
Of the 58 million motor vehicles in the world, Russia had three million, and the U.S. had well over 40 million. If everyone in the U.S. took a car ride at the same time, each car would have less than five people on average.

OCTOBER
With the exception of agriculture, the auto industry was the largest occupation group in the U.S. Approximately 20 percent of the total national income was earned by people engaged in automotive and kindred pursuits.

APRIL
On the 50th anniversary of the auto industry, 25.5 million cars were on the road. In 1896, there were only 16 cars registered in the U.S.

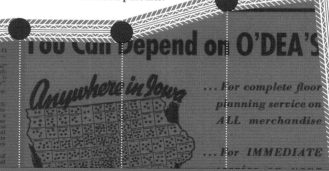

1946   1948   1949

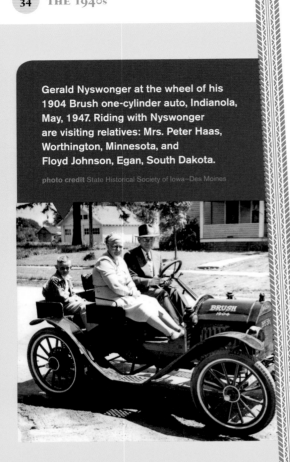

Gerald Nyswonger at the wheel of his 1904 Brush one-cylinder auto, Indianola, May, 1947. Riding with Nyswonger are visiting relatives: Mrs. Peter Haas, Worthington, Minnesota, and Floyd Johnson, Egan, South Dakota.

photo credit State Historical Society of Iowa–Des Moines

Model T
IN USE IN 1947

"Some folks say the Old Model T will outlast all other cars. But this 1904 Brush is making a bid for the title. Owned by Gerald Nyswonger, Indianola, this 43-year-old, one-cylinder Brush still putts along fine on its own power. Nyswonger drives it to Des Moines occasionally and finds it excellent transportation. Nyswonger says he picked it up in a junkyard 10 years ago, made a few repairs and started driving it. He obtained the 30-inch by 3-inch tires from a mail order store (Sears). The frame and axle are made of wood; there is a chain drive; it has only high, low and reverse gears with no clutch; and the one-cylinder runs left-hand. There's no crankcase. Oil is fed by an old-fashioned glass-bulb dripper. Nyswonger gets 30 to 40 miles per gallon of gasoline, held in a four-gallon tank. The whole car weighs only 800 pounds."

–May, 1947, State Historical Society of Iowa

When dealers were again allowed to sell their inventory, only people involved in certain professions were eligible to purchase them. Those individuals included physicians, surgeons, visiting nurses, farm veterinarians, practicing ministers, persons engaged in fire fighting, persons needing automobiles for police work, other public health and safety workers, and those who transported produce to and from farms.

IADA Helps the Cause

In April, 1942, IADA's secretary-manager, Ray Spatz, completed work on the association's convention and ended seven months of employment with the organization to enter the Armed Forces. That month NADA used the state associations to set up a "battalion of automotive men for immediate action," to serve primarily as auto mechanics, but also as guards and police, typists and clerks, tool room keepers, machinists, electricians, and firemen.

In conjunction with NADA, C.A. Morris, Iowa's NADA director from Waterloo, was asked to set up a Permanent Military Committee for Iowa. This committee made recommendations to the War Department of Iowa of automotive personnel with mechanical skills and officer capacities. By July the War Department requested IADA's help in setting up another maintenance battalion. Meanwhile, Americans wondered how essential and aging vehicles in their communities were to be kept running without qualified mechanics to handle repairs. During the war years, auto mechanics became one of 34 classes of essential workers in the U.S. Iowa dealers repeatedly fought their local draft boards for deferments to keep their knowledgeable mechanics on the job in their communities.

At the same time, the IADA worked to interpret the regulations issued non-stop by the federal War Production Board (WPB), Office of Production Management (OPM), Office of Defense Transportation (ODT), War Management Commission (WMC), Office of Price Administration (OPA), and Reconstruction Finance Corporation (RFC). The task was overwhelming. Some of the initial regulations accumulated 100 amendments during the war years. These amendments corrected flaws in earlier orders and allowed for changes in available resources and conditions in the fighting overseas. One monthly issue of the *Bulletin* might contain three amendments to a single regulation.

Many times IADA called upon dealers to scour their facilities and counties for scrap iron and steel to use in the production of tanks, ships, guns, and other war materials. In 1942, more than 25 percent of all scrap produced in the state came from worn-out automobiles and trucks. In addition, since Japan controlled much of the world's rubber supply, every dealer and driver looked for ways to preserve tires.

A "relief bill," the Murray-Patman Law, was signed in mid-1942. The law allowed dealers to choose either RFC loans or the purchase of their frozen new car inventories. Loans on new cars in stock were at cost plus one percent a month for carrying charges. If dealers decided to liquidate, they could turn their cars, trucks, and tires over to RFC at laid-in cost, plus a reasonable charge for expenses to the date RFC took them. The maturity dates on loans, originally set for 18 months, were extended as the war went on.

In July, 1942, the WPB reported that the automotive industry was devoting 95.1 percent of its efforts to direct war production. During the war the industry turned out $28 billion worth of war products, equal to one-fifth of all armament output. Although dealers weren't free to carry on business as usual, IADA reported that the majority of its members were "carrying on. ... They have found new and scattered sources of income, and reduced expenses to the minimum."

National gasoline rationing became effective November 11, 1942, not only to conserve fuel, but to preserve precious tires, parts, and batteries. Soon after, hours were set for the operation of service stations.

IADA's directors, who had been trying to run the association after Spatz left in April, 1942, hired former dealer and IADA field representative V.E. Laurence in September of that year to be secretary-manager and continue field work. Bernyce Stilwell, the Des Moines office manager, handled the task of *Bulletin* production.

Lt. Ray Spatz wrote that the First Battalion of the 301st Ordinance Regiment landed in North Africa the day after Christmas, 1942. Attached to a supply headquarters, Spatz reported that he was "scouring the country for used automobiles." His wife wrote that "in company with an interpreter he was buying up American made cars, of which he says there is a surprising number. ... All the Iowans are in good spirits, interested in the country, but anxious for the end of the war and another glimpse of Iowa's rolling prairies."

In March, 1943, auto rationing was "liberalized," and the nation's stock of 240,000 new cars was available to "government exemption permit holders or certificate holders, legally capable and financially able to buy a car." Iowa's quota of passenger cars was 1,058 in May and 987 in August. By November only 75,000 new cars were left in

Vern Nall

"The larger part of our livestock is sent to markets in nearby states by trucks, because rail transportation has not been sufficient, and we have 642 towns that have no railroad facilities. There are 975,000 cars and trucks in the state of Iowa, and over 70 percent of these are in the hands of food-producing farmers, and the average age of the farm car is 7 years. If the automobile dealers are not able to service and repair and keep running this 70 percent of these automobiles and trucks devoted to agricultural production, the production and transportation of food will be immediately and seriously curtailed in the greatest food-producing state in the union. ... We believe there is no more reason for freezing the stock of used cars than for the freezing of horses and mules, in the hands of livestock dealers."
—Vern Nall, IADA vice president from Iowa City, who traveled to Washington, D.C., in January to protest the freeze on auto sales at a hearing in the House of Representatives, from the February, 1942, *Iowa Automobile Dealers Bulletin*

In 1946, dealers were preparing for a post-war boom of the industry. Many dealerships were building new showrooms, including Orville Lowe's dealership (top photo) at 524 East 6th Avenue in Des Moines. Construction began in 1949 on Allen Motor Company's new building in Cedar Rapids. Pictured (bottom photo) are R.H. Allen, Leonard Roman (building superintendent), A.W. Allen, and R.W Rinderknect (contractor).

photo credit (top photo) State Historical Society of Iowa–Des Moines

dealer stocks nationwide. In 1943 some 33 million cars and trucks were said to still be operating, so just under 2 million vehicles disappeared from U.S. roads during 1942.

Used cars, which had been the bane of automobile dealers until World War II, now became their salvation. Prices continuously went up. Pre-war, dealers strained to get a 30-day used-car turnover to avoid losses. Now dealers found themselves in a rising market, which meant more profit the longer they could keep the units.

Individuals who didn't have legitimate dealerships frequently bought and sold used cars. This complicated the situation. In Blackhawk County from August 1 to 11, 1944, 129 used cars were sold, but only 20 of those were sold by dealers. While state legislation generally was not a priority during the 1940s, IADA worked with the Dealers Licensing Division of the Department of Public Safety to propose a regulation with a new, stronger definition of "a place of business" for a dealership.

Regional Meetings

On August 10, 1943, some 40 members of the Northwest Iowa Automobile Dealers were called together by IADA President Walter Mahoney of Sioux City. "During these times when we cannot travel so far it was decided that a get-together in this part of the state would be helpful," Mahoney said. Other dealers followed suit, with meetings attended by a few dozen dealers in neighboring counties. This regional meeting concept stuck. At the end of the war, a traveling team of IADA leaders and state officials spoke at dinner meetings attended by approximately 100 dealers (the maximum most facilities in the state could accommodate for a dinner meeting) representing eight to ten counties. By the end of the decade, IADA was successfully holding 18 sectional meetings per year.

The Automobile Trade Association Managers credited IADA with originating the "district dealer meeting" as a strategy to build and hold "a wise association membership and carry on an active program." As the decade ended, IADA planned to run these meetings from June to December, with six to eight speakers representing IADA, NADA, and key state agencies.

By mid-1944, with Allied invasions underway, IADA told members that some men being released from military service might have experience in motor vehicle repair and could soon be available for employment. Rumors began flying about how soon new-car production would resume, "especially if there are any widespread cutbacks in military production." But by March, 1945, the need to continue heavy production for the war with Japan following European VE Day gave "no encouragement" on the hoped-for production of new cars.

As War Efforts Wind Down

In February, 1945, the Bulletin began carrying news about significant growth for dealers. That growth included Ford's construction of a $700,000 service parts building in Des Moines, designed to address dealer needs in 81 counties. It also included announcements of sales and purchases of dealerships, and expansions of their buildings.

George Means, who had served as supervisor of dealer registrations for Iowa's Motor Vehicle Registration Department and worked with IADA on strengthening the

Marion County Mailmen
CHOOSE JEEP

L. Eldon Thornburg, a U.S. Postal Service rural mail carrier had a 52-mile route that included 28 miles of completely unsurfaced roads in Marion County. "Under wet conditions he often delivered his mail on horseback when road travel by Model-A wasn't possible," says his son, Leland. "My father enlisted in the U.S. Navy during the war and had a personal mission of his own during that time of service to his country." Eldon Thornburg wanted to save enough money to purchase a jeep to use on his mail route when he was discharged. Mission accomplished: he purchased his first jeep in February, 1946.

"Dad's new experience with his jeep was a positive one and he quickly passed the good word on to the other Marion County rural mail carriers," he says. Others quickly placed their own orders for new jeeps. The Thornburgs, who lived in Pleasantville, had five jeep products from 1946 to 1950.

Rural mail carriers stand proudly beside their own war-proven vehicles at Knoxville during the winter of 1947–48. Eldon Thornburg is fourth from the right.

dealer licensing law in 1945, became secretary-manager of the association in August, 1945. V.E. Laurence continued to serve as IADA's field representative. All 1942 model-year automobiles were eliminated from rationing in August, 1945.

In September, 1945 the Bulletin's cover simply read "Peace." The 1946 IADA convention was attended by 678 "enthusiastic auto dealers, more than double the number that had ever attended a state dealer meeting."

Post-War Problems

After the war, auto parts were scarce, production was slow, and auto owners were advised to "continue to nurse their present autos longer." Selling prices were still being controlled, and the average car on the road was eight years old and had been driven 56,000 miles—compared to 1925 when the average car ran for six and a half years and registered 21,750 miles.

In 1945, factories were producing some 1946 models, but many plants were still converting equipment back to automobile manufacturing. Post-war production was impacted by labor strikes for higher wages, shortages of production materials, and inability to get supplies and parts from vendors when they were needed on the production line. By January, 1946, the auto industry had made just 142,367 post-war cars, and by November automobile dealers had an estimated 5 million unfilled orders for cars. Retail orders in 1947 were two times production expectations.

Consumers who were fortunate enough to get a new car from one dealer's waiting list were tempted to profit by taking a second or third car when their names came up on other dealers' lists. They could resell those cars immediately at higher prices. In July, 1947, about half of Iowa new car dealers were contracting with purchasers not to sell their new car for six months—except to the dealer from whom they bought it. This "repurchase option agreement" started in Virginia, was utilized in many states, and was tested in the courts in Oklahoma.

A Car from the Last War

"Teenagers glow with envy when C.G. Rankin, Cedar Rapids, drives by in his good-as-new, bright blue 1918 model Overland touring car. This ghost of by gone days is still in perfect order." It has only 12,000 miles and tires "as good as any today." The 27-year-old car hadn't been driven in 18 years "until Rankin discovered it jacked up in his neighbor's barn" and purchased it for $75. Fees and extras of $50 readied it for Rankin to drive to work. Rankin's son (stationed with the Air Force in Austria) and members in his outfit had a "hot controversy raging" over whether or not the car—which had a tank three-quarters full of 'aged' gasoline—would start. "It all resulted in several small wagers being placed, G.I.'s being G.I.'s even in Austria." Just a little tuning and it started up. Even with tires "bright red as was the style in the last war" and a motor "a bit noisy by modern day standards," Rankin says he wouldn't take $1,000 for the car. "And who can blame him? In these days even a car from the last war is valuable—if it runs."
—Walter Navin, September, 1945, *Iowa Auto Dealers Bulletin*

Still without enough cars to sell, dealers wanted the government entities set up for wartime controls to expire and the "ill-advised and ridiculous" industry regulations to end. IADA passed a convention resolution for the post-war freedom to operate without "orders and regulations which are so voluminous, complex, uncertain, unrealistic and frequently arbitrary that an automobile dealer cannot engage in the every day transaction of business without unwittingly violating one or more of such regulations, even though he exercises the utmost good faith, care and diligence."

In June, 1946, Tom Coughlin, Coughlin Sales Company, Davenport, wrote to his senators and congressman. His territory, he said, had a quota of 135 cars per month. But since the first new 1946 Hudson rolled off the assembly line the last week of August, following V-J Day the summer before, the entire territory had been shipped less than one month's allotment. "Keep, if you wish, certain controls, but take them out of the hands of dictators with

The White Way Auto Company, founded in 1917 in Pella's opera house building, had a fire on January 16, 1948. An open house at the rebuilt showroom included musical entertainment among the cars and farm equipment. The dealership sold Chevrolet and Olds.

no knowledge or sense of fair play, and whose greatest concern is to perpetuate themselves in present positions."

On November 10, 1946, the auto industry was free of government control. IADA President Paul Pritchard wrote, "I urge every new and used car dealer in Iowa to hold their prices to good business procedure. The lower we can keep our prices now when we have no inventory, the less they will come down when our stocks are good. Some of the profit we could make will pay a greater dividend in customer goodwill."

Legislation in Iowa

World War II interrupted regular state legislative sessions, and most battles were fought with national regulations. But in 1945, S.F. 151, which became effective July 4, represented two victories for Iowa auto dealers. It strengthened the definition of a place of business in Iowa's dealer license law, and it increased fees to provide funds to investigate reported cases of improper dealings. There was controversy over the need for a strong Certificate of Title law in Iowa to "make fraudulent deals practically impossible." In 1949, S.F. 180 limited the maximum penalty for operating without an automobile dealer's license to a $100 fine or 30 days in jail.

Welcome Home, Veterans

To celebrate the homecoming of local soldiers, J and R Motor Supply of Davenport cancelled all debts owed by 700 returning service men as a victory gift, which amounted to approximately $10,000. Iowa Motor Company, an Oelwein Ford dealership, was approved as a mechanical training center for veterans. Five veterans began working at a training school at Henaman Motor Company in Estherville. On-the-job training programs became law for both disabled and qualifying able-bodied vets, and four vets went to work at Schwertley Chevrolet (no town given) as part of that program. In addition, the 20,000 disabled Iowa war veterans who had lost limbs were to get specially fitted, free cars through a $30 million government expenditure. By January of 1947, 27 of every 100 people employed in the nation's auto industry were vets of World War II.

People

From June, 1944, to November, 1948, the "association officers" listing in each bulletin included Roy H. Allen as NADA Iowa director. Frank Collord is identified with that position in December, 1948.

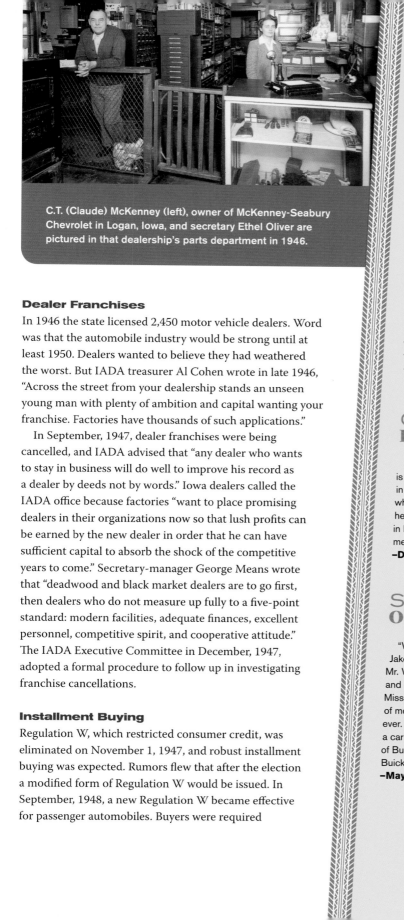

C.T. (Claude) McKenney (left), owner of McKenney-Seabury Chevrolet in Logan, Iowa, and secretary Ethel Oliver are pictured in that dealership's parts department in 1946.

Dealer Franchises

In 1946 the state licensed 2,450 motor vehicle dealers. Word was that the automobile industry would be strong until at least 1950. Dealers wanted to believe they had weathered the worst. But IADA treasurer Al Cohen wrote in late 1946, "Across the street from your dealership stands an unseen young man with plenty of ambition and capital wanting your franchise. Factories have thousands of such applications."

In September, 1947, dealer franchises were being cancelled, and IADA advised that "any dealer who wants to stay in business will do well to improve his record as a dealer by deeds not by words." Iowa dealers called the IADA office because factories "want to place promising dealers in their organizations now so that lush profits can be earned by the new dealer in order that he can have sufficient capital to absorb the shock of the competitive years to come." Secretary-manager George Means wrote that "deadwood and black market dealers are to go first, then dealers who do not measure up fully to a five-point standard: modern facilities, adequate finances, excellent personnel, competitive spirit, and cooperative attitude." The IADA Executive Committee in December, 1947, adopted a formal procedure to follow up in investigating franchise cancellations.

Installment Buying

Regulation W, which restricted consumer credit, was eliminated on November 1, 1947, and robust installment buying was expected. Rumors flew that after the election a modified form of Regulation W would be issued. In September, 1948, a new Regulation W became effective for passenger automobiles. Buyers were required

First Automobile
TRACED TO 1875

"Boston (UP)—A 96-year-old Back Bay man is credited by the Massachusetts Council of Automobile Old Timers as the builder of what may have been the nation's first automobile. George A. Long constructed a charcoal-burning motor vehicle at Northfield in 1875 consisting of a chassis on wooden wheels with a fifth wheel in front for steering and a solid axle to which the driving wheels were keyed. He got his idea from an army camp in New Hampshire where he saw a steam boiler and visualized steam as the source of propulsion for his vehicle. The Long car was sold to a railroad which replaced the wooden wheels with train wheels and used the vehicle to carry newspapers to Keene, New Hampshire. Patents were obtained by Long in 1883 on a two-speed, 300-pound 'steam road vehicle' which made the first use of the ballbearing steering fork still used on bicycles."

–March, 1947, *Iowa Automobile Dealers Bulletin*

Oldest
IOWA DEALER?

"A 93-year-old automobile dealer in Humeston, Iowa, is claimed by Ford officials to be the oldest active dealer in the United States. He is Joseph E. Doze, who served as a Democrat in the Iowa Senate when he was 79. Doze, who is still selling cars, was greeted in Des Moines by Ford officials attending an annual meeting of 250 Iowa Ford dealers."

–December, 1946, *Iowa Automobile Dealers Bulletin*

Speaking of
OLD TIMERS

"We had the pleasure of a visit the other day from Jake Weitzel of the Weitzel Motor Company, Atlantic. Mr. Weitzel has been a Buick dealer since 1912, and claims to be the oldest Buick dealer west of the Mississippi. Jake was overflowing with optimism, banks full of money, crops good, says a new 1946 Buick is the best ever. He remembers in 1913 when Walter P. Chrysler was a car salesman, and Charles Nash was president of Buick. Weitzel Motor Company now has the agencies for Buick and Pontiac in Atlantic, Iowa."

–May, 1946, *Iowa Automobile Dealers Bulletin*

It's Different NOW

"'When can I get a new car?' is today's $64 question. But the clamor for cars is in marked contrast to the 'demand' following World War I. Then, the question wasn't 'when', but 'how much?' For, over 74 percent of the makes retailed above $1,500, with nearly a fourth of those priced above $3,000. Most generally purchased, though, was a touring car which looked something like a bathtub with seats. Closed cars were available only at high prices.

The problems of where to drive and how to get service always confronted motorists in 1919. Compared with today's 1,406,366 miles of surfaced rural highways, only about 10 percent of roads were paved. Gasoline stations were a novelty, not yet affording the thorough fueling, minor repairing and all-round servicing found in today's 241,000 enterprises. Parts and equipment were expensive, too. A 30 by 3½ fabric tire cost $16.80, and it had no tread. With a tread the price was upped to $20, while a cord tire with a tread cost $37.50–for a small size.

Still other economic differences in the automotive world set apart the two periods. In 1919, only 340,000 people were employed by the industry. In 1946, plants are planning to employ more people than at any time in history, with expectations well above the record high of 517,000 workers. Registrations of vehicles also graphically records the changes. Slightly over 6,770,000 passenger cars were licensed then, as against 25,500,000 cars on the road now."
–April, 1946, Iowa Automobile Dealers Bulletin

to have a down payment of at least one-third of the total purchase price. If the unpaid balance was $1,000 or less, the maximum maturity was 15 months; if more than $1,000, it was 18 months. Installment payments were not to be less than $70 per month.

NADA immediately went to work, as dealers began reporting that customers found it impossible to put one-third down or make payments of $70 per month. The national association called for auto dealers to send in specifics so they could build a case against these "oppressive controls." NADA believed that every third car prospect failed to buy because of the hard terms of the new regulation. Eventually the law was relaxed. The one-third down stood, but with longer loans and smaller monthly minimums. These changes were followed by an increase in both new car sales and financing.

As the Decade Closed

By 1948—the year the auto industry built its 100-*millionth* vehicle—only eight states had more hard-surfaced roads than Iowa, and the state ranked fourth in the nation in number of miles of concrete roads. Nationally, dealers were getting an average of seven automobiles a month from factories. The average car was now being scrapped at 12 years old and 100,000 miles. While car owners tried to hang on to what they had, the safety of aging vehicles was a concern. Replacement parts were being turned out at triple the pre-war peak rate so that millions of older cars could be kept in operation. Record production of new cars still hadn't caught up with the orders on dealers' desks.

IADA's 1948 convention was attended by "700 men and 100 ladies." They elected directors from Iowa's eight congressional districts to add to the association's executive committee. "Their advice and counsel will be appreciated," the newsletter said. The association called upon dealers to help identify individuals who were violating the Dealer License Law. Believing that "each community should clean its own house," the IADA began taking confidential information and passing it along to the Dealer License Division to investigate violations. The IADA *Bulletin* frequently listed the names of violators and their fines, and later would carry statistics on the number of dealers licensed and the number investigated.

IADA Services

IADA began the Automotive Collection Credit Bureau in 1947 to help members with collection problems. On September 29, 1948, IADA's Executive Committee voted to make group insurance a service to its members and named Bankers Life Co. as the underwriter for life, hospital, and surgical insurance. The "insurance coverage which we offer our membership can not be bought at a lower net cost from any other source," the newsletter said.

In 1949, IADA had 2,064 members, the largest in the association's history. Even so, it did not rank "too well" in respect to NADA membership. The IADA *Bulletin* warned, "The end of the present lush times for the automobile dealer, if not in sight, is at least nearer at hand."

Post-War Customer and DEALER RELATIONSHIPS

"In 1946, after the war, my son-in-law, Bill Cramblit (IADA president in 1956), returned from the armed services in Europe (an army captain). I took Bill into the business as a partner. ... Our hardest problem for several years was to deliver the new cars we received in the proper order as the car orders had been received. There was a terrific demand for new and used cars; also, we had five sub-dealers to whom we furnished cars. Many, many times, we were offered hundreds of dollars on the side above the regular car prices for immediate delivery. We did not accept any of this at any time. This was pressure selling in reverse, and it took a lot of time to explain to a friend or customer why he would have to wait for his turn on the list in the delivery of a car, and then only at the regular price."
– Lester Glover, Wapello County, who began his 50 years as an automobile dealer in 1919 (from *Fifty Years in the Automobile Business,* written in 1969)

G. O. Fletcher

"The average individual is willing to pay for a car but he isn't willing to see a dealer make a terrific profit on the customer's used car and is not willing to take this gracefully. He remembers and so can a good many of us the terrific loss that occurred on used cars and the terrible 'cut-throat' business that we had due to the fact that we had a used car problem. Today we do not have this used car problem and a few dealers are taking advantage of this situation at the expense of future relations. Some have said that in the future a $10 or $25 differential will get the business so why not take as much as the traffic will bear right now. This is not an equitable situation."
–G.O. Fletcher, IADA president, December 1947, *Iowa Automobile*

A PLEDGE FOR 1946

As an Automobile Dealer, I Pledge Myself and My Organization . . .

1. To be worthy of the trust imposed in me as a representative of the world's greatest industry;

2. To serve the motoring public to the best of my ability, always delivering fair and full value and being ever mindful of my responsibility;

3. To so conduct all my affairs as to win the plaudits of all the business men of my community to the end that I may be regarded with that respect to which my position entitles me;

4. To so operate my business that other automobile dealers may regard with respect and admiration the honest, fair, and clean competition which my organization provides;

5. To do all within my power to protect and advance the general use of Motor Vehicle transportation and to promote a greater degree of highway safety;

6. To constantly keep before myself the objectives for which all business is organized . . . namely, the rendering of a service for fair compensation, realizing that sound management and constant application will produce an ample reward.

More than 80 percent of the nation's automobile dealers were NADA members in 1946 when NADA wrote: "The entire 42,000 new automobile dealers in the U.S. are being unfairly smeared by the shifty sales practices of a minority of the trade."

PICTURE BRIGHT ONLY FOR AIR LINES

By George Mills

Copyright 1944, reprinted with permission by The Des Moines Register.

There is real concern in high places over the possibility that a transportation crisis may be in the making for Iowa and the whole United States.

Much of our war-accelerated civilization is rolling on equipment that would have been junked long ago if these were peacetimes. Virtually no new vehicles are to be had for civilian use.

The heavy tire situation is bad. Government officials say there are trucks out of service in Iowa right now because tires can not be procured. The supply of automotive parts, however, is improving.

Everywhere are hints that the jams on trains may force the government to institute travel rationing in some form. Rail passenger business, already at undreamed-of heights, is continuing to expand and buses are loaded to capacity on weekends and at other times.

Space for Wounded

Complicating the problem on trains is the need for space for wounded members of the armed forces. It may be necessary for the government to take over passenger trains to transport the wounded heroes from the battlefields of Normandy, Spain, and Italy, some government officials have hinted. This probably would be done only as a last resort and only if civilians who insist on taking pleasure trips monopolize passenger trains.

More plane seats

Only in the air is the picture brighter. The air lines are getting some of their planes back from the government and it isn't nearly as difficult to obtain a seat on a westbound plane now as it was a few months ago. Eastbound air traffic hasn't been too heavy for some time and there always has been plenty of plane space, relatively speaking, north and south out of Des Moines. Plane officials got a big kick out of booking a railroad official through to Denver when his own line was unable to take care of him.

The railroads, however, report that they are handling all the freight business that comes their way without too much difficulty. Freight volume seems to have tapered off somewhat compared with a year ago, rail officials said, probably because of a downward tendency in defense shipments.

Car Shortage

The rail car situation is tight right now because the bumper wheat crop is beginning to move in the southwest.

Maintenance of over-age and over-loaded equipment is a problem taxing transportation authorities. The labor shortage is the principal difficulty in that field.

For example, the Rock Island railroad is using 20 women in an all-Negro crew laying rails near Walcott in eastern Iowa. The 53 men in the crew are given the heaviest assignments but jobs in that kind of a project didn't used to be considered suitable for feminine workers.

Bus line officials report their biggest maintenance problem is to find time to keep the buses off the road long enough to service them.

Both bus and city transit lines lack experienced drivers. And everybody seems to need competent mechanics.

State tax commission figures indicate that Iowa right now is at least 175,000 new automobiles and trucks behind its normal peacetime purchases. The last new cars to be sold to all comers were distributed in the final months of 1941.

Few New Cars

The commission figures 85,000 new vehicles were sold in 1941 in this state. Under rationing restrictions, new car and truck sales dropped to approximately 20,000 in 1942 and to about 8,000 in 1943. And the curtailment has been even sharper this year. For example, the office of price administration (OPA) has a new car quota of only 28 passenger vehicles for July in the 64 counties of the Des Moines district.

In June the quota was 40 and in May 95.

"The average automobile on the road today is seven years old and 25 percent of them are beyond 10 years old," was the comment of Dale Shaw, state superintendent of motor vehicle registrations.

"The average car is past the usual age of junking. Its efficiency is not over 60 percent."

Shaw reported that car registrations in this state will not exceed 600,000 this year, compared with 717,000 in 1941. Thus, more than 100,000 cars have been taken off the road in this state since Pearl Harbor and all the rest are more than 2½ years older.

Less Mileage

The superintendent pointed out however, that gasoline rationing and car conservation practices adopted by owners have greatly reduced the average mileage traveled.

"Trucks, on the other hand, are being used more intensively than ever before," he said. "They're taking a real beating but their owners as a general thing are keeping them up well."

Donald R. Wigdon, office of defense transportation (ODT) chief for the Des Moines district, reported that of the 33,500 trucks in his 33 counties, 51 percent are 1937 models or older.

Aged Trucks

Fifteen percent are 1931 models or older, his figures show. That means about one out of six trucks in the district is at least 13 years old.

Widgon reported that about 10,850 of the truck units are being used in agricultural work. In this group also more than half the trucks were seven or more years old and 24 percent were 1931 models or older.

It is axiomatic that the older a motor vehicle the more expensive it is to keep in operating condition. There is no choice now but to keep them going or to do without transportation facilities.

> "Much of our war-accelerated civilization is rolling on equipment that would have been junked long ago if these were peacetimes."

Widgeon said only 10,048 truck units were produced for civilian use in 1943 and 80,000 are scheduled for production and delivery in the last half of 1944.

"This 80,000 may be compared with normal prewar replacement production of 450,000 a year," he said. "It is imperative that truck operators exercise all possible care in preventive maintenance and in driving habits. In most cases their present trucks probably will be the last which they will be able to obtain until the end of the war."

Wearing Out

John Kamerick, newly appointed regional rationing officer in the Chicago OPA headquarters, said: "Cars are going off the road at the rate of 5,000 a day to the junk pile and as this number is bound to increase in the coming year, due to the age of cars and the inability to obtain parts, it is reasonable to expect our rolling stock will fall to 20 million cars over the nation by next July 1."

He said there were 27 million cars on the highways in early 1942.

"Unless truck operators reduce their speed, discontinue the abuse of tires by overloading and take to using recaps, there is no doubt but that a third of all vehicles will be off the road within the next 90 days. We are faced with the most critical truck tire situation so far in this war," Kamerick said.

Gas Rationing

He predicted that gasoline rationing will continue "until after the Japanese war ends" but said larger rations may be expected "very soon" after the German war is concluded.

John Gillespie, executive secretary of the Iowa Motor Carriers association, said, "all trucks are three years older now, have been put to the utmost use and naturally are strained almost to the breaking point."

Meanwhile the railroad passenger trend continues upward, especially on the usually jam-packed streamlined trains. On the North Western-Union Pacific trains, it takes as long as 30 days to get a reservation to the west coast and it is a two- to three-weeks proposition to line up a reservation to Denver.

The Rock Island reported that "it is useless to ask for any reservations west under 30 days."

Another railroad report said that "litter cases" of wounded men "are getting pretty thick" and "that type of passenger is just starting." Litter cases always require a drawing room on a train.

Bus line officials said the traveling public "is very tolerant and patient."

Polite Public

"I think many of these people are so nice because they are conscience stricken," he commented. "They know they shouldn't be traveling at all now."

Discontinuance of the use of Camp Dodge for selective service inductions saved the bus lines running to Des Moines from a bad summer of record-breaking throngs, the sources said. Even so, the lines have about all the business they can handle, particularly on weekends.

The United Air Lines is getting six planes back from the government and it tentatively has scheduled an extra flight each way east and west beginning Aug. 1 through Des Moines. That addition would give this city five flights a day west and six east.

Missing Cars

J. M. Bann, assistant general freight agent of the Rock Island in Des Moines, said his railroad has only 10 percent of its own cars on its line "and we won't see the others until the war is over." He said freight tonnage is heavier proportionately in the east than it is out here.

George Langworthy, North Western freight agent, said the manpower shortage has been intensified "by these unending washouts this year." He agreed that the shipping situation now is "a bit easier" than it was a year ago. He said the railroads are "vastly more efficient" this war than they were 25 years ago.

Russell Reel, head of the Yellow Car Co., in Des Moines, said his company is doing an all-time record business right now with the same number of cabs it was using in 1942.

City street car and bus lines in Iowa are carrying double the passenger loads of 1938. For nine representative cities, the 1943 total was 96 million passengers, compared with 44 million in 1938.

The usual problems of parts, tires, drivers and condition of equipment confront transit line operators.

Part of the transportation crisis facing Iowa and the nation is due to the fact that the flow of automobiles to the junkyards continues unabated while no new cars have been made since 1941. Here is the automobile junkyard of the Capital Auto Parts Company, Forest Avenue and Illinois Street in Des Moines.

OBEY ALL TRA

While mandatory driver education legislation was not enacted in the 1950s, IADA members supported such programs and provided vehicles for use by schools throughout the state. Two Des Moines East High School students are shown turning in their driver safety examinations for a driving class.

photo credit State Historical Society of Iowa–Des Moines

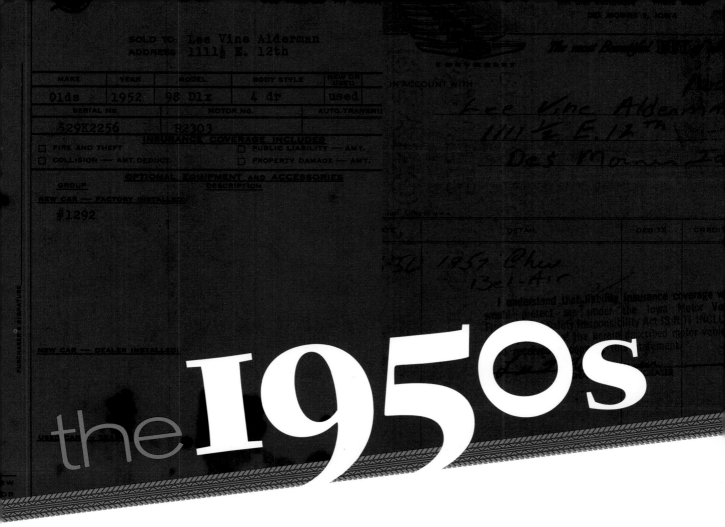

the 1950s

"We can't afford to have the automobile taxed out of existence. A common fallacy existing in Washington and throughout the nation is that the automobile is a luxury item. It is an educational responsibility of the automotive trades to get people in authority to understand that the automobile is essential to modern living."

–Alfred Kahl, September, 1951, *Iowa Automobile Dealers Bulletin*

Thirty Years of Automotive PROGRESS REVIEWED

"The automotive industry's march of progress is reflected in a recent review of the 12 present makes of U.S. passenger cars whose ancestors were on the road in 1920, according to Lee Thomas.

'The review, recently completed by the Automobile Manufacturers Association, reveals that the price of four-door models today averages nearly $900 less than in the so-called good old days. In terms of industrial wages, this price decline is even more impressive. It takes only 34½ weeks to earn the price of today's cars, where it took 92½ weeks back in 1920. Moreover, horsepower has been more than doubled. In fact, even the most expensive models, which were selling at more than $5,000 back in 1920, had less horsepower than the lowest priced cars on today's market.

'During this period, hundreds of refinements have been added by all makes. These include the all-steel body, four-wheel hydraulic brakes, safety glass, built-in luggage compartments, coil spring suspension, automatic spark advance, sealed-beam headlights, weather-insulated body construction, windshield wipers and many others.

'Finally, the life span of cars 30 years ago numbered 25,000 miles compared with the many cars today that have over four times that mileage. Americans know value and, considering these facts, it's no wonder that demand is keeping pace with record new car production.'"

–May, 1950,
Iowa Automobile Dealers Bulletin

Before the end of 1950, the Korean War was underway, and IADA secretary-manager George Means had died. Alfred W. Kahl—the Iowa Commissioner of Public Safety—was named to replace him. Consumers feared a freeze on new motor vehicles with the onset of another war. But while there were occasional parts and accessory shortages, along with wage and employment issues during the 37-month conflict, the impact on Iowa's auto industry was minimal by comparison to World War II.

The financing restrictions of the "revised" Regulation W affected car buying until the Defense Production Act of 1950 was amended in 1952. The credit restrictions were "the most drastic economic regulation ever forced upon a free people," according to Fred L. Haller, NADA president. With 549 people killed on Iowa highways during 1949, IADA members continued their interest in safety. Concerned that financing controls had kept more old and unsafe automobiles in operation, they promoted public safety inspection efforts and "led the nation in safety programs." In 1951 in the Quad Cities, five dealerships—Vincent J. Neu, Inc., Strieter Motor Co., Schwind-Boeker, Inc., Dahl Motors, Inc., and Quality Buick—helped form a salvage company as a safety measure to get rid of junk cars. To further promote safety in the 1950s, IADA supported legislation for mandatory drivers' education in high schools (not enacted in 1950s), provided automobiles for school systems to use in teaching (valued at more than $500,000 by 1955), and supported dad-to-daughter and man-to-man good driver programs for parents and young drivers.

MARCH
First-year depreciation on new cars in 1949 was 3.5 percent per month. Before the war, vehicle depreciation was 22 percent per year.

OCTOBER
In October, Iowans paid the state nearly as much money in gasoline tax as they did for all of 1924. Revenue from gas tax was more than 12 times higher in 1950 than in 1924.

APRIL
The first year that IADA published a Dealer License Directory, it included an alphabetical listing of all businesses in the state that had received an auto or truck dealer license.

SEPTEMBER
IADA promoted a "civil defense motion picture" entitled *Escape Route,* a 20-minute "sound color film available for dealers to take to civic groups." It emphasized the "importance of the automobile in escape from a wartime emergency."

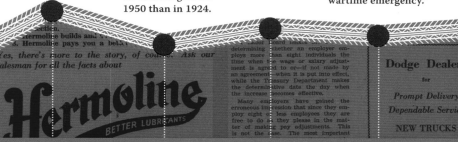

1950   1951   1952   1955

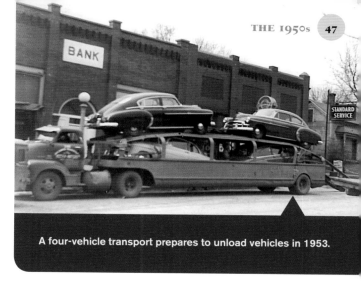

A four-vehicle transport prepares to unload vehicles in 1953.

NADA

At the beginning of the decade, Frank Collord of Waterloo, a past president of IADA, continued to represent Iowa within NADA. In 1956, he was named regional vice president for NADA, and in 1957 he was elected to his fourth three-year term as state NADA director.

In 1950 NADA began sponsoring fall membership drives, known as GAD or "Give a Day" to NADA. IADA leaders throughout the state recruited new NADA members, and their efforts paid off. IADA took top national recruitment honors in 1951, 1954, and 1959, when they added more than twice the number of members to the national rolls than the second-place finisher. The Iowa association placed second in 1952.

The relationship and respect between IADA and NADA was reciprocal, as Iowa dealers worked with NADA for legislation such as the O'Mahoney-Cellar "Good Faith" bill, which defined a franchise and limited manufacturers' control of dealers, and the Monroney-Priest "bootlegging" bill.

When the NADA annual meeting was held in Washington, D.C. in 1956, IADA members, who were no strangers to contacting their congressmen to express their viewpoints, went together to Capitol Hill for the first time.

IADA Membership

As the decade began, membership in IADA was relatively high, but 400 Iowa dealers still had not joined the association. IADA moved its membership drive to the spring. By the end of the decade, it was mailing dues statements in November and receiving record numbers of checks in the next batch of mail.

After 10 years without a change, the IADA increased dues for 1953. The membership fees ranged from $17.50 for sellers of two to 99 cars and trucks to $60 for those selling 200 or more vehicles. In 1953, only 200 Iowa dealers were not members of IADA, and 35 counties had 100 percent membership. In 1955, 94 percent of eligible dealers were members, with only 100 "free riders," according to Al Kahl. In 1954, the state had 1,618 dealers; by 1958 that number had dropped to 1,247. While membership was down by almost 400 dealers, Iowa had virtually the same number of non-members as it had in 1953.

An associate member classification began appearing in 1953, and IADA quickly had more than 100 associate members—primarily finance companies and banks.

Member Services

In 1951, IADA began publishing "Flash Facts" for time-sensitive alerts and renamed its monthly magazine the *Iowa Auto Dealer*. Drawing on industry news from other publications, the magazine included reports from state dealer associations, legislative wrap-ups, county and community member news, NADA news, conference promotional materials, post-event summaries, and news of IADA services and district meetings. Nearly every month, condolences marked the passing of dealers past and present. "Flash Facts" became so useful that IADA began publishing a "Ready Reference Guide" every six months to compile the mailings into one resource.

By mid-1951, the association's group insurance program covered more than 1,000 dealers' employees, with total claims averaging $1,200 per month. In 1952, the group insurance program was revised to provide hospital benefits, polio coverage, and paid time off for sickness. In the first six months of the revised program, $21,000 was paid out. The program added deluxe options in 1954, and by 1957 the plan included diagnostic x-rays and laboratory fees. Ten "dreaded diseases" were added to the coverage in 1956, the same year the name "IADA Services, Inc." became official. By January, 1959, dealers had received more than $550,000 in benefits since the program's beginning. In the first six months of 1959, claims averaged more than $10,000 a month.

"We are transportation merchants selling transportation rather than motor vehicles. We want to sell safe transportation, but under today's conditions the safety factor is not improving. ... We don't have roads adequate to serve today's automobile traffic. Our present road program is, to my mind, just a patchwork project. If there is [a road plan] it is so tied up in politics that no one not in high office has any idea what is proposed."

R.E. McCoy

—R.E. McCoy, IADA president, March, 1952, *Iowa Auto Dealer*

In October, 1958, after several years of study and careful analysis, IADA launched a workers' compensation program and provided the coverage required by Iowa law at an "absolute minimum cost" of 15 percent below manual rates. As the "owners" of the program, participating dealer members received additional dividends if the loss ratio was less than 56 percent of the gross annual premium. Some 300 charter members—the number needed to implement the program—quickly signed on, and by November the program was underway.

IADA continued to add essential services for dealers. By 1952, for instance, 75 percent of members were using the association's collection service. In 1955, the association published a Sales Tax Guide and Record of Used Cars and Trucks book, helping dealers provide accurate tax reporting. The book addressed 425 used car transactions, and the Iowa Tax Commission said it "would go a long way toward simplifying sales tax audits and in minimizing misunderstandings." IADA began studying the addition of a forms service for members in June, 1953, and in May, 1956 offered a repair order form, new car invoice, and used car invoice. In 1957, IADA added the Iowa retail installment contract to its offerings.

Honorary Members

In 1952, IADA bestowed its first lifetime honorary membership on William Wissler, president of the Herring-Wissler Company, a Des Moines wholesale auto parts firm, and the 1923 president of the Iowa Automotive Merchants Association, the IADA's predecessor. Wissler called the

Elected at the 1956 convention were (seated) Lee Thomas, president; Bill Cramblit, first vice president; (standing) Dale Norton, second vice president; and C.L. Dickerson, treasurer.

recognition "one of the biggest thrills of my life." In 1956, honorary memberships were presented to C. A. Morris of Waterloo, Elmer Dunn of Des Moines, and Howard Sole of Des Moines. William Culver was selected for honorary membership in 1958, and in 1959, R.N. Archie, B.C. Hawn, and W.B. Swaney were so honored.

Conventions and Meetings

Julian A. Peverill

By 1950, there was a national Automobile Old Timers (AOT) group—for persons in the business for 25 or more years—and the oldest dealer in point of service for Iowa was listed as Julian A. Peverill of the Hudson Jones Automobile Company of Des Moines. Peverill was listed as a past president of the Des Moines and Iowa automobile dealers associations in his family's account of "The Peverills and the Automobile: Iowa's Largest Automobile Distributor, 1906–1952." IADA's records do not show that he ever held that state office. It is, however, stated in the *Iowa Automobile Dealers Bulletin* (July, 1932) that "The state of Iowa is fortunate in having a director of the National Automobile Dealers Association, Mr. J.A. Peverill, a well-known automobile distributor of Des Moines." Peverill's first franchise, obtained in August of 1907, was for the Regal car.

The Hawkeye Chapter of AOT, which had 3,829 members nationwide in 1951, began meeting annually in connection with the IADA spring conference. Leaders early on were C.F. Claiborne, L.J. Brady, Clarence Schukei, C.E. Mace, and Chet Carmer.

While these industry elders enjoyed their own gatherings, NADA began a Young Execs group for the future leaders of the automobile retailing industry. In Iowa, the program was headed by Warren McEleney, Clinton's 1951 Young Man of the Year and, at that time, the youngest president to lead the Chamber of Commerce of Clinton. In the 1950s, these Old Timers and Young Execs groups held concurrent luncheons at the IADA conventions.

In 1951 promotional material for the IADA convention, president R.N. Archie, said, "Next to the Sidney Rodeo, I believe that our state convention this year is going to be about the best affair you can possibly attend." That year, G. Verne Orr of Pasadena, California, the group's second president in 1920, sent a message to those attending: "Please extend greetings to your banquet guests. It might interest younger automobile men to know that the principal objective of officers and directors in 1920 was to

Cars, as Well as Corn
ONCE PRODUCED IN IOWA

"Iowa is seldom thought of as a center for automobile production, but in the past 60 years, eight different makes of cars have been manufactured here. This interesting fact, along with thousands of others, is listed in a booklet recently published by the National Used Car Market Report, Inc., a Chicago, Illinois, firm.

The first car manufactured in Iowa was the Adams Farwell, which had a brief life. This car was made in Keokuk in 1904.

The Colby was made at Mason City from 1911 to 1913 by the Colby Motor Co., and the L-C-E was manufactured at Waterloo in 1915-16. Two other makes were put out in Waterloo by the Mason Motor Company.

The most successful car manufactured in the state, from the standpoint of years of production, was the Spaulding, produced at Grinnell from 1913 to 1917." ...

"The final car made in Iowa was the 'Iowa,' about which little apparently is known. This car didn't even rate the brief records listed with most of the passenger cars, and only the name, 'Iowa,' is listed.

The booklet says that since the inception of the automobile industry, in 1890, 1,775 different brands of passenger cars have been in manufacture. Only 21 of those makes are now being produced, and only 12 of those were being manufactured 40 years ago.

The oldest listing given in the booklet belongs to the Orient, which first came out in 1890. It was manufactured in Waltham, Massachusetts. One of the most recent listings in the booklet is the Playboy, produced only in 1947 in Buffalo, NY."

Some of the other facts listed in the 1950's book:

- *Nine out of ten passenger cars in this country are used each week for purposes of earning a living.*
- *During an average week, 73 percent of the nation's private cars are used for traveling to and from jobs, conducting business or doing work on the farm.*
- *Shopping during the week puts 53 percent of the cars to work.*
- *A total of 22 million passenger cars are used every week for earning a living while 16 million are used for shopping.*
- *Forty-five percent of all employed persons use a passenger car in connection with their work.*

–January, 1952, *Iowa Auto Dealer*

The Spaulding automobile was manufactured by Spaulding Carriage and Automotive Works from 1910 to 1916. At the height of production the company was Poweshiek County's largest employer, with nearly 400 workers. According to the Iowa Transportation Museum being developed in Grinnell at the Spaulding's factory, the assembly line rolled out 1,481 automobiles. The medium-priced cars sold for $1,500 to $1,600. "While the cars were stronger, more powerful and more luxurious than Ford's Model T, the company was never able to achieve true assembly-line production capability and could not charge enough for the cars to remain profitable. By 1929, it was all over, and the buildings were occupied by other companies."

photo credit State Historical Society of Iowa–Des Moines

make illegal the sale in Iowa of any bobsled or sleigh with less than 56-inch tread. None was wider than 48 inches then. When roads were broken through snow it seemed important to us that automobiles be able to use the same track. After legislative meetings in ten different parts of the state with all lawmakers we could assemble, proper legislation was passed. That made the year successful." With 850 dealers at the convention and 1,350 at the fall district meetings, 1951 set a record for meeting attendance.

The conventions became grand events for dealers, with more national speakers, teaching skits, extravagant evenings of entertainment, and popular ladies' programs. The convention wrap-up in 1951 stated, "The ladies attending the convention weren't forgotten. Each one who registered was given a beautiful compact, and a luncheon

IADA's 1958 convention was chaired by M.O. (Bud) Kahn (center). He's pictured with luncheon speaker Richard L. Wilson, director of *The Des Moines Register* and *Tribune's* Washington News Bureau, and Iowa Governor Herschel Loveless.

In Allen Motor Company's new building in Cedar Rapids, every mechanic was provided with a twin post hydraulic hoist and overhead reels for air, water, and trouble lamps. The "masterplate" concrete floors were "skid proof and dustless." Radiant heat in the floors was used throughout the entire building, and the temperature was controlled by inside and outside thermostats.

and style show for the ladies was held at Younkers tea room." In 1953, the number of dealers in attendance was slightly lower, but the number of wives doubled. Throughout the 1950s, dealers registered for $15 and their wives for $10.

Both the convention and the dealer meetings used an informational "clinic" concept during the 1950s. At the district meetings, an afternoon clinic was added to dispense information on a particular topic—complying with a new regulation, completing required forms, and answering specific dealer questions. Dealers began to bring their office managers, bookkeepers, and auditors to these sessions. Private "line-make" meetings were added to pre-convention activities in 1956 and district meetings in 1957 to allow members to "discuss common problems without exposing their own practices or problems to competitive dealers."

Legislation

In 1952, more than 800 dealers took part in an IADA survey regarding the need for a Certificate of Title law in the state. Some 758 reported they had never sustained a loss on a transaction involving a stolen car, and 590 reported that they did not regularly check with the county recorder (for lien status) when acquiring a used car. The IADA group studying the issue felt that dealers were evenly divided and recommended no official action. But in January, 1953, IADA's legislative committee approved a Title Law bill drawn by staff and legal counsel Tom Roberts and presented it to the House and Senate Motor Vehicle Committees for consideration. According to IADA, it was developed as "a dealer bill" and would "not add to the present work load of dealers in their business." It passed "word for word" and took effect in October, 1953.

In 1955, IADA successfully pushed for legislation that put a tariff on "bootlegging" of cars and changed the definition of "used car" to include the words "has been sold at retail," benefiting the legitimate franchised dealers.

In 1958, IADA sought to prohibit Sunday sales of new and used cars because "all auto dealers cannot afford to assume the 10 to 14 percent increase in personnel costs that appear to be inevitable if all dealers are forced by competition to remain open on Sunday." Public opinion was favorable, and the action was viewed as good public relations. The legislature approved, and prohibition of Sunday sales and advertising of autos went into effect July 4, 1958.

Thomas Roberts

"I recall that when I was first approached about becoming the association legal counsel I was told that the principal reason I was being offered the job was that 'a young lawyer is all the association can afford.' Because clients were none too plentiful in those depression days of the early thirties I readily accepted the association's offer and soon found that this aspect of the job had not been misrepresented. My modest retainer fee, which was supposed to be paid on the first of each month, was seldom forthcoming on that date. ... I recall that in those early days when Walter Ferrell, who was then secretary-manager, and I appeared before a group of dealers, Mr. Ferrell would introduce me as the association's new 'general counsel.' This high-sounding title made up to a considerable extent for the lack of regularity in my compensation."
—Thomas B. Roberts, IADA Legal Counsel, on his 25th anniversary as IADA's legal counsel, March, 1959, *Iowa Auto Dealer*

Protection Strategies

In 1952, IADA's executive committee approved a long-range plan of action to combat future problems that were likely to confront the state's dealers. Their "protection" objective included improving relationships with government, employees, the public, and the industry.

That year IADA began promoting NADA's Get-Out-the-Vote campaign to serve communities, provide goodwill, and address public relations. Local citizens needing rides to the polls in November could get them from local auto dealers. That program won IADA a special citation from NADA and was offered again in 1956, with 500 dealers taking part. The auto industry fought image issues and fraudulent advertising and sales practice problems for much of the decade, and both IADA and NADA developed codes and standards in response.

To best understand employee relations, IADA surveyed dealership employees regarding a variety of working conditions. The association's 1959 dealer meeting theme—"Put Your House in Order"—addressed the findings.

As the decade closed, IADA began developing a Guaranteed Warranty (G-W) sticker. Under this innovative program, participating dealers guaranteed a discount of 15 percent on all cash purchases of labor and parts on a G-W used car for one full year from the date of purchase at the dealership. The association also added a staffer, Kenneth Newcom, as insurance consultant to help members analyze policies and coverage needed by an automobile dealership.

By 1954, Al Kahl's efforts to move the association forward had earned him a title change to executive vice president.

Sue Corley, Des Moines, in front of IADA office, ponders over the idea of getting a free ride to the polls on November 4th, 1952.

Reminiscing... Elmer Henaman RECALLS THE MAXWELL

In an interview for the *Estherville News*, Elmer Henaman, an IADA director for 20 years, reviewed the days when "the [car] body had to be removed to get to the two-cylinder engine of a Maxwell." Henaman had been connected with the automotive business for 46 years by 1959, but his son and son-in-law operated the Henaman Motor Company from which the elder Henaman had retired.

"Elmer entered the auto business as a dealer in 1919 at Armstrong after having been employed by a dealer for more than six years. His first cars were the Chandler, Dart, Liberty and Essex, and he handled these makes until receiving a Ford franchise in 1922. For the past 37 years the firm has handled Ford, and has been located at Estherville since 1933.

"'I have had many amusing experiences,' he says. 'Once was after I sold a car to a customer, we headed the car out the door. The customer drove into the street, but kept the car in a cramped position and circled in the street several times. Finally he headed for Silge's Harness Shop, where we finally got him stopped. His front wheels were inside the window of the shop and horse collars were hanging all over the radiator.'

He also recalled the arrival of freight car loads of Model T Fords.

"'I have unloaded freight car loads of Model T's, all knocked down with seven in a car. We had to assemble them and prepare them for sale. In those days we had no gravel roads or snowplows to open the roads. One winter we delivered cars by bobsled to farmers...I taught many of the people to drive when they purchased a car in those days.'"
–December, 1959, *Iowa Auto Dealer*

Idea SHARING

"Our good friend, Paul Millians, vice president of Commercial Credit Corporation, who has addressed many automobile dealer conventions, recently talked to the Canadian Automotive Wholesalers Association convention; and one of the points he brought out seemed so important that we are passing it on to you:

'There was a time when businessmen thought the thing that made them great was their secrets. But as they got together—trade organization, conventions—they found that the wall built around their business kept more good ideas from the outside than it kept in. A business seldom improves when there is no other model but itself to copy; and we are not smart businessmen if we don't ride part of the way on the experience of others; because about the biggest business folly of them all is attempting to solve problems others have solved—not identical perhaps, but basically the same.'"
–July, 1950, *Iowa Auto Dealer*

Iowa Automobile Dealers Association 415 Tenth Street / Des Moines 50309 / Tele

June 26, 1968

TO: All IADA Members.

1. Enclosed is the July Tax Tickler which we failed to enclose
last Flash Facts.

2. ACTION REQUESTED IN OPPOSITION TO H.R. 17748.
In Flash Facts of June 14 we urged you to contact your Congress
(Senators & Representatives) in opposition to H.R. 14816. A subst
bill that is almost as bad has come out of Committee and may be ac
upon in Congress within the next 10 days. The number of the
is H.R. 17748. It gives the U.S.Secretary of Labor power to
all businesses with respect to "Safety and Health".

Although you may not be acquainted with the full content of thi
highly undesireable bill, may we assure you that it is dangerous a
merely creates further federal bureaucracy. We alrea
able and unjustifiable set of safety rul
shop. To permit the Federa
business under

CRESCENT CHEVROLET CO.
SALES SERVICE

EXIT

CHEVROLET

CRESCENT

In 1964, Crescent Chevrolet was located at 5th and Keo. The sign shown on the
right side of the building was the first Chevrolet sign sold to a dealer after World
War II. The sign traveled with the company and was retired when the dealership—
the last of the downtown auto dealers—was sold by Bill Jensen in 2007. Jensen,
who started as a 17-year-old car jockey at the company in 1949, took over
ownership in 1980 from Jim Piggott.

FROM GUARANTEED WARRANTY

dds are 513 to 1 against you without a warranty

GW

SERVICE BULLETIN No. 2

-- IMPORTANT ANNOUNCEMENTS TO ALL GW DEALERS --

Within a day or two you will receive a huge white envelope with the following wording on the outside: --

Mr. Dealer, do you realize you could have been held liable for damages and repairs caused by alleged mechanical defects on every car sold last year unless you specifically stated in writing the specific warranty limitations on each car sold?

If you were an average dealer last year, you sold 513 used cars, you did not offer some kind of warranty with each car sold, 513 opportunities to have a lawsuit. Here's why — Under the Uniform Commercial Code, in effect in practically every state, on each and every used car that you sold...

the 1960s

"In many cities disguised factory dealerships have replaced all or almost all independent dealers of two companies. In large cities and the urban areas surrounding them, factory financed dealerships are becoming the rule rather than the exception. This trend is accelerating at such an alarming rate that many dealers are certain their days are numbered and within five or so years all will be eliminated in one way or another. All of this is happening, not because the retail sales are lagging, but because subsidized selling is being used as a means of increasing a company's share of the markets. ... The Good Faith law (1956) must be and will be replaced by a franchise bill which places upon the manufacturer the burden of proof, and which does not have other weakness of the Good Faith act. ... Is it too much to ask that the great corporations be required to act in a non-discriminatory, fair and equitable manner?"

–Alexander Hammond, a New York attorney specializing in cases involving dealers resisting franchise termination, speaking at the 1969 IADA convention, second quarter, 1969, *Iowa Auto Dealer*

Auto Men Embrace GUARANTEED WARRANTY (G-W) PROGRAM

"There is one very good reason why we like and are using the G-W: OUR CUSTOMERS LIKE IT! They like it for a number of reasons; first, being issued through the IADA they have confidence in it; second, it is good at other dealers in cities other than our own; third, it covers items other than those included under our old 50-50 guarantee; fourth, it is good for one year, regardless of mileage. And, also important, our salesmen like it because it gives them a good selling tool."
–John Whittaker, Whittaker-Long Ford Sales, Inc., Council Bluffs, July, 1960, *Iowa Auto Dealer*

"I entered the G-W program last January with very little enthusiasm. In fact, I wasn't much sold on the idea. However, I am now convinced it is a good, sound used car merchandising aid. It looks to me like there is real, permanent value in the G-W program and it will help solve the warranty problems with used car customers."
–Al Eisenman, Eisenman Motors, Inc., Grinnell, July, 1960, *Iowa Auto Dealer*

"We are 100 percent sold on the G-W program. There is a lot of integrity and prestige behind it that the customer likes. We write each used car buyer a personal letter explaining the warranty and enclose the G-W certificate and the 'dealer list.' We have the customer sign the certificate when he gets the car but fill it out and mail it to him later, along with our lube ticket and the personalized letter that I mentioned. Wish more dealers would get into this program—it is the best answer I have found to the used car warranty problem."
–Dick Evans, Tate Cadillac-Olds, Waterloo, July, 1960, *Iowa Auto Dealer*

One of the IADA's greatest successes in the '60s was the Guaranteed Warranty (G-W) certificate program, which kicked off in January of 1960 with 500 Iowa dealers participating. This warranty program was expected to boost customer confidence in used cars by providing a 15 percent discount on cash purchases for repairs made to pre-selected vehicles on the dealer's lot. Dealers soon reported that the program resulted in a reduction in the volume of unpaid warranty work done on all used cars. The program caught on outside of Iowa and before the end of the first year, more than 100 South Dakota dealers had signed on, Wisconsin dealers were set to start, and Nebraska dealers were meeting to add the warranty program. Iowa's G-W emblem of identification was consistent throughout the program and became recognizable in participating states.

Within two years, the program was active in 11 states and the province of Ontario, with 3,300 dealers participating. IADA's 1961 president Bud Kahn credited the program with "bringing back to the dealers some of the quick service work which the dealers should never have lost" to service stations and specialty shops. The *Saturday Evening Post* carried a G-W advertisement in October, 1962, and by 1963, 10,000 dealers were participating in 37 states and six Canadian provinces.

Frank Potts, association president in 1962, credited the program with raising the image of IADA from coast to coast. Potts, Kahl and goodwill ambassadors Bud Kahn, Bill Fletcher, Johnny Lujack, Ray Allen, Don Cornelison, and Karl Jorde spoke about the program at meetings throughout the nation. The program continued and was enhanced in November, 1966, when a new G-W certificate, valid for a 24-month period, was introduced.

Dealer Image

Public image was an issue for auto dealers. In 1960 a record nine auto dealers sought public office, and eight of them won in the primaries. Grundy Center auto dealer W.L. "Bill" Mooty became Iowa's lieutenant governor, and five others were elected to the legislature. Seeing the value of people in high places who understood the automotive industry, dealers continued to help get voters to election locations. Fort Dodge dealers made 100 new cars available to transport voters to the polls in November, 1960. They issued a "Get Out the Vote" challenge to other dealer organizations in cities with populations of at least 25,000 to see who could get the highest percentage of registered voters to the polls on Election Day.

IADA surveyed members in 1962 and circulated its findings: Franchised auto dealers in Iowa rated high as substantial businessmen and civic-minded community leaders. The survey showed that the typical auto dealer had a capital investment of more than $100,000, met a payroll of about $45,000 per year, and put an additional $20,000 per year into circulation in his community for other business expenses. Collectively, the investment of Iowa auto dealers was nearly $100 million; they contributed $60 million a year to their hometowns through wages and local purchases; they employed 14,000 workers; and they provided a living for 40,000 persons in the state. At least 90 percent of dealers took part in local charity drives, and 93 percent were active in Boy Scouts, Red Cross, Salvation Army, YMCA, and other community organizations. Approximately 50 percent had been or were involved on their church boards and had held public office.

Iowa lieutenant governor William Mooty, an auto dealer from Grundy Center who previously had served as a representative in the Iowa legislature, and Clark Mullenhoff, *The Des Moines Register* Washington correspondent, at the 1964 IADA convention.

"Without the IADA, we as individuals would not be able to withstand the encroachment of government into our business, and we would have no success in gaining concessions from the factories if we work only as individuals."
—Lee Holt, IADA president, at the 1968 IADA district meetings where he declared that every auto dealer should get involved in the process of self-government in his city, the state, and the nation, Winter, 1968, *Iowa Auto Dealer*

"Orville Lowe (center) and Jim Vail of Mid-Town Motors, and Ken Newsom of IADA smile with enjoyment as they look over a reprint of a full-page advertisement which is appearing in the October 20th issue of the *Saturday Evening Post* as a national boost to the Guaranteed Warranty program which now stretches from coast to coast in the United States and reaches into six Canadian provinces. Lowe's Mid-Town Motors is the newest Iowa member of the G-W program."

Nationwide Advertising
SUPPORTS G-W PROGRAM

"More than 8,000 dealers participating in the Guaranteed Warranty program in the United States and Canada will see their used car sales warranty program promoted by the use of a nationwide advertisement in the *Saturday Evening Post*.

In addition to the national advertising by the magazine, another push with an expected nationwide effect took place at the National Auto Show at Cobo Hall, Detroit, which began October 20, 1962.

The national advertising will be backed on the state level by the appearance of a two-color advertisement in *The Des Moines Register* of Sunday, October 21, on the outside page of the state section. This will list the 540 GW dealers and the message will be carried to some 550,000 families."

–September–October, 1962, *Iowa Auto Dealer*

Safety Pays

Attention to safety paid off for IADA. In 1960, the association was one of 11 states honored with an achievement award by the Insurance Institute for Highway Safety for promoting the high school drivers' education program in 1959-60. Iowa dealers were furnishing 475 cars to high schools, with 203 provided without cost to the school, and another 272 in programs in which schools shared the cost of the car.

IADA president Norman Dunlap called for auto dealers to get behind state seatbelt safety in 1966 and named an IADA seatbelt chairman in every county. During the 1966 IADA convention, hundreds of auto dealers signed up to participate in the Auto Dealers Traffic Safety Council to demonstrate and promote dealer support of traffic and auto safety programs at the local level. IADA convention-goers passed resolutions to support "Buckle Up for Safety" and statewide inspection of motor vehicles. In 1967, they distributed vehicle safety kits to more than 600 schools, clubs, and other prospective sponsors. For two consecutive years, IADA was honored by the Auto Industries Highway Safety Committee for its participation and support in safety-related matters.

Services

In addition to concerns about public safety, Iowa dealers focused attention on safety programs for their employees. They worked to keep workers' compensation rates low and earn dividends in the form of reduced rates. Each dealership elected a safety chairman, and IADA provided materials to help identify and correct hazards and practices that might lead to accidents. The IADA workers' compensation program was "in the black" by 1961. That year IADA participants were paying at a rate of 88 cents per $100 of payroll earned, instead of the base manual rate of $1.03.

When a workers' compensation rate increase came in 1964, IADA absorbed it and continued to push for higher membership participation in its program. That year, dealerships began earning safety awards from Iowa's industrial commissioner Harry Dahl, state labor commissioner Dale Perkins, and IADA. Gold certificates went to firms that had at least three successive years in which the claims paid from industrial accidents were less than 25 percent of the premiums paid, silver certificate

awards went to firms that maintained a loss ratio of less than 40 percent for two years, and bronze awards went to firms with a loss ratio less than 60 percent of premiums paid for two years.

In 1969, dealers taking part in that IADA program learned that safety paid big dividends. They received $28,000 in 325 checks, more than 20 percent of the 1969 earned premium. This put some firms' payments for 1968 at just a little over half the 1968 standard manual rate for workers' compensation coverage in Iowa.

IADA's group health insurance program had not increased rates since the program began late in the 1940s. About 1,600 people were covered early in the '60s. The program added 28 firms and 360 employees in 1961, and by 1962 had paid out more than $1 million in benefits since its inception. Without increasing costs to participants, additional benefits were added in the early '60s, including family group life insurance. By early 1966, the amount paid out since the program started topped $2 million. As the decade ended, the program was paying out at a rate of a half million dollars a year.

Membership dues were not used to subsidize any IADA service. In fact, IADA Services, Inc. was keeping membership fees in the "lowest dues bracket of any state association except one." In 1961, total income from dues was $35,136 (excluding convention expenses and revenue), and the association's operating expense was $40,396. Funds from group insurance administration ($6,981) and IADA Services ($2,900) kept IADA from going "miserably in the hole." In his final president's report in early 1961, Don Cornelison said, "If we did away with all of our service programs to the members it would be necessary to raise our dues at least another 25 percent to meet the absolute minimum expenses necessary to operate the affairs of IADA."

In 1962, IADA added "Tax Ticklers"—a reminder of taxes due each month—to "Flash Facts," and member Bill Boshart wrote, "Al—The only thing better than your 'Tax Ticklers' would be the abolishment of taxes."

Forms available through IADA proved valuable for the members. Membership stayed high—typically nearly 1,100 members—throughout the '60s, when 90 to 98 percent of eligible dealers were association members. The "built-in" chattel mortgage on the IADA Repair Order form was not obtainable in any other standard repair order.

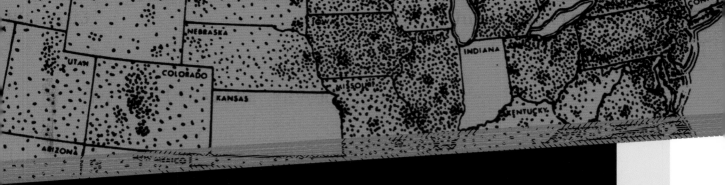

Kahn Talks About Auto Industry
TO NEWSPAPER PERSONNEL

Editor's Note: Below is a portion of a presentation made by M.O. "Bud" Kahn to present the dealer point of view to a group of newspapermen.

"If you study the record of the last four years you will see a very interesting development. The automobile industry is not just maintaining an eight-million-car level. It has been climbing up, steadily and vigorously, by at least half-million-unit steps, year after year. And there is nothing in view which would indicate any possibility of stumbling as it takes the next step in the year ahead. All the reliable indicators lead us to believe that in 1966 the industry stands a very good chance of equaling and possibly even surpassing the 1965 all-time record for retail delivery of automobiles.

Here are six reasons why I think so.
1. From now on through the 1960s, nearly four million youngsters a year will reach age 16, the driving age in most states. They will provide a steady pressure of additional demand for automobiles, new and used.
2. There is a clear trend toward an increasing number of multiple-car families.
3. The expansion of the nationwide system of freeways should continue to provide a stimulus for car ownerships.
4. The annual scrappage rate for cars is now up to between the five and six million mark; just replacing those scrapped cars puts us well on the way toward more high volume years.
5. The state of the economy and the confidence of the people was never better.
6. The factory emphasis on new styling, safety and gadgets (particularly air conditioning) will stimulate sales.
    These six factors make any auto dealer look to the future with optimism."

Kahn stated that the auto dealer has two basic problems: sales and expenses.

"First, let's talk about expenses. The auto dealer probably handles more money for the least amount of profit than any retail businessman in the world. The average profit (before taxes) on sales over the past six years is 1.8 percent, which means that for every $100 worth of sales, the average auto dealer's net (not gross) profit before taxes is one dollar and eighty cents. Now, let's be kind to your local hometown dealer and say he is a hot-shot and made two percent, or two dollars on every $100 worth of sales. Now if he wastes, or doesn't spend wisely, only $5, he must do $250 in sales to get that $5 back. This brings home the importance of expense control. I know of no other dealer in your hometown that actually has to watch his expenses as does the auto dealer.

So, if a dealer turns you down on a $5 ad, and you think he is a cheap so-and-so, please remember that he has to do $250 in sales to get that $5 back. That is five valve jobs, about 23 motor tune-ups, or 165 grease jobs. Be a little understanding now that you know more about the importance of making every advertising dollar count."
–M.O. "Bud" Kahn, a past president of IADA, in a speech before the classified advertising section of the Iowa Daily Press Association, September–October, 1965, *Iowa Auto Dealer*

"The automotive business seems to be booming—and we certainly are looking forward to another record-shattering year in automobile sales. The automobile manufacturers are chalking up all kinds of records—and there are predictions that these records can be shattered again in 1966. This is good news for the industry.

It is less than cheering, however, then to note that the NADA Business Management survey shows that dealer profits for 1964 (1.8 percent of sales) were an even smaller part of the sales dollar than they were in 1963 (2.8 percent of sales)—which in turn was smaller than 1962.

The emphasis then must be on the part of management to manage for profit. I am certain that we agree with those who say, 'The business of business is profit.' But, the mere fact that we are in business will not guarantee us a profit, nor do I think that we can be assured of profit unless we devote time and management to the creation of a satisfactory profit from our operations."
—**Howard Howlett, IADA President, convention report, March 29, 1965, *IADA Directory***

In 1964, IADA began NADS of Iowa—the IADA Warranty Service program—a new car warranty program that was a franchisee of National Auto Dealers Services. Designed to help dealers receive all the reimbursement for new car warranty services to which they were entitled, the program kicked off in August with a limited number of dealers and newly trained staff members. Headed by former State Center auto dealer Bob Miller, the NADS staff processed 563 claims in the first eleven days of August. The average claim was $17.26, the largest $326, and the total reached $9,717. By 1965, claims were being processed at a rate of 3,000 per month.

IADA was ready with a "Weekly Locator" service when a favorable revision of the trade-in tax credit rule went into effect in January of 1965. The service let dealers notify fellow members about makes of used cars or used trucks they might wish to sell or buy. By that time, though, used cars were not enough of a problem to make the program necessary.

In 1965, dealer Mert Coover wrote a letter to IADA supporting the association's Automotive Credit Protection Bureau, saying he didn't usually write endorsements. Coover had tried five or six different services of that type over 14 years and found them to be ineffective. But in just three years the Automotive Credit Protection Bureau had collected "a sizeable amount of money from accounts we had charged off as bad debts and skips."

In 1966, IADA Services added electronic data processing to provide "dependable accounting services at an economical cost" to both large and small dealerships. In early 1967, IADA Services began offering a credit life

program through Reliance Life Insurance Company of Illinois. This insurance coverage for car buyers was offered "to relieve families of financial responsibility at the time of loss of the family head."

More than 1.5 tons of paper—factory-required accounting and service forms—rested on newly installed shelving in an IADA Services warehouse near the office in 1967. IADA put these forms in members' hands quickly, at low transportation costs, and with a discount for prompt payment.

In 1969, Marv Hartwig, IADA president, noted that the association's dues structure had been unchanged for four years. This had "been possible because of income derived from quality services, performed by a top-notch staff at a lower cost to the dealers than could be obtained elsewhere. Now, however, with the burden of ever-increasing expenses being thrust upon our association, it is essential that we seek additional income if we are to maintain our sound economic status. This can be accomplished only if more dealers use the services offered by IADA."

Outstanding Volunteer Leaders

In 1960, Frank Collord, who had served for 12 years as Iowa's NADA director and chaired the national group's personnel committee, decided not to run again, and C.J. Murray, Sioux City, took a term to represent the state before he retired from the auto trade.

Honorary members added in the 1960s were E.E. Wheeler of Waterloo, Walter Mahoney of Sioux City, A.B. Chambers of Des Moines, Don Cornelison of Atlantic, W.L. Mooty of Grundy Center, Paul Pritchard of Mason City, C.J. Murray of Sioux City, Frank Collord of Waterloo, and R.E. McCoy of Carroll.

In 1966, Warren McEleney, who had been speaking at NADA management seminars around the country in the early '60s, was elected Iowa's NADA director and regional NADA vice president for Iowa, Wisconsin, and Illinois. He joined the NADA executive committee and was named trustee to the NADA retirement trust. In 1968, he became NADA treasurer and chair of the important Industrial Relations Committee of NADA. In late 1969, McEleney was elected first vice president of NADA and was slated to assume that office in January, 1970.

During 1966, when more than 98 percent of the licensed new-car dealers in the state were IADA members, the association's president was Floyd E. Hughes, Jr., the "first of the 'second generation' presidents" of IADA. His father headed IADA during 1934–35.

In 1963, IADA officers were Karl Jorde, president; Howard Howlett, first vice president; Norman Dunlap, second vice president; and William Fletcher, treasurer.

In 1969, Marshalltown's John Rude, who served as the first president of IADA in 1919, was chosen "Honorary President" of the newly created Past President's Club of IADA. Lee Holt, immediate IADA past president, was named president of the newly formed group.

Conventions

The 1964 convention must have been a solemn gathering. The night before it began, legal counsel Thomas B. Roberts died of cancer. At a memorial service on Monday of the convention, the dealers remembered the man who had served IADA since 1934. Before the end of the decade, IADA would present three scholarships in Roberts' name to young Iowans—sons of member employees who were interested in becoming automotive technicians.

"In Iowa, the automotive sales and service businesses employ nearly one out of five persons of the state's entire retail, wholesale and service business working population. Over 40 percent of all Iowa state tax collections are special motor user taxes such as license fees, gasoline tax and sales and use taxes. In addition, Iowa motorists paid $63 million in federal excise taxes on motor vehicles, fuel and parts last year. ... Automotive retailing is one of the few retail sales businesses that still remains under the ownership and control of a hometown citizen. The reason gigantic chains and discount houses have not moved into the car sales field is because the investment is too big and the risk is too great for the financial returns that can be realized. The auto dealers of Iowa owe it to themselves and to their customers to inform the public of the importance of having locally owned car sales and service businesses for every major make of car in every reasonably populated Iowa community. And they must be financially sound, well-equipped with specialized tools and parts and manned by highly trained service technicians if we are to enjoy safe and economical transportation for the future."
—Al Kahl, IADA Executive Vice President, November-December, 1961, *Iowa Auto Dealer*

The 1960 IADA convention featured a "Night in Las Vegas" for dealers and their wives. Desert Inn posters decorated the walls of the Hotel Fort Des Moines. Lively entertainment and drawings for such prizes as luggage were part of the annual gatherings.

Golden Anniversary OPEN HOUSE

Robert Beck, editor of the *Centerville Iowegian* in 1966, attended the golden anniversary open house at Carmer Motor Company. He visited with Mr. and Mrs. Charles Carmer and Mrs. Chester Carmer, widow of the company founder, "Chet" Carmer, who served as IADA president in 1952. Here is an excerpt from the column Beck wrote.

"In 1916 when Chet, as he was called by his friends, started the business, he was 20 years old. It was a different day, a different age when large capital outlays were not required to enter the automotive business. The automobile business was still in its infancy, gaining more and more acceptance, but certainly still competing with the horse and buggy. On any given day in Centerville in the year 1916, the horses and buggies that were hitched up around the square outnumbered the parked automobiles.

Imagine a 20-year-old youth going it on his own and entering the automobile business today! Even if he possessed an unusual ability, good available capital and assuming that he could even get a franchise, his chances would be mighty slim.

Chester Carmer, however, entered the business when it was in its infancy and grew with it. It was in rented quarters before the day of trade-ins. He not only had to sell a car, but teach people how to drive. The gear shifts were rather complicated to novices and if you didn't know what you were doing, you could strip the gears. I recall that my own mother warily decided to learn how to drive, stripped the gears, and abandoned the project.

In those early days, the dealers had to drive to Detroit to pick up their new cars. Now transports deliver them to the dealer's door. Mrs. Carmer recalled that Chet bought an extra heavy fur-lined coat for winter driving. The old touring cars had side curtains that you could place on the vehicles, but they were not too satisfactory and car heaters were not in use. A winter drive from Detroit to Centerville was something of an ordeal, over mud roads for the most part.

While Chet was still getting his feet on the ground, he found himself locked within the Great Depression. Unless you have been a part of this experience, it is difficult to understand the seriousness of this great economic debacle, how searing the results, how it has affected all who passed through those days. My own business career was launched while this depression still raged, and the imprint remains."

Mr. Beck closed his column with the following observation: "Today the automotive business has reached an age of maturity. But there is little doubt that if it is to survive for still another 50 years it will face many changes just as it did in the last 50. Circumstances may be altered. Opportunities are greater than ever. But it will require some business acumen, good service, sound management, astute promotion for any firm to grow and survive in the next half century."
–January–February, 1966, *Iowa Auto Dealer*

This shot of an Iowa group visiting FBI director J. Edgar Hoover was probably taken in the early 1960s during an NADA convention. Pictured are Frank Potts (1962 IADA president), D.J. Cornelison (1960 IADA president), Mrs. Al Kahl, Mr. Hoover, Mrs. Frank Potts, Mrs. D.J. Cornelison, and Mr. Donovan Day.

"In many cities disguised factory dealerships have replaced all or almost all independent dealers of two companies. In large cities and the urban areas surrounding them, factory financed dealerships are becoming the rule rather than the exception. This trend is accelerating at such an alarming rate that many dealers are certain their days are numbered and within five or so years all will be eliminated in one way or another. All of this is happening, not because the retail sales are lagging, but because subsidized selling is being used as a means of increasing a company's share of the markets. ... The Good Faith law (1956) must be and will be replaced by a franchise bill which places upon the manufacturer the burden of proof, and which does not have other weakness of the Good Faith act. ... Is it too much to ask that the great corporations be required to act in a non-discriminatory, fair and equitable manner?"

—Alexander Hammond, a New York attorney specializing in cases involving dealers resisting franchise termination, speaking at the 1969 IADA convention, second quarter, 1969, *Iowa Auto Dealer*

In 1965, Al Kahl, who was hospitalized following surgery early that year, was released to attend one evening of the convention. His health required a second surgery and a transfusion, and Kahl developed infectious hepatitis. His recovery took months away from his passions at IADA.

The Hotel Fort Des Moines continued to be IADA's convention location. In addition to hearing top industry headliners each year, IADA members welcomed Senator Barry Goldwater in 1961, Paul Harvey in 1963, and *The Des Moines Register's* Pulitzer Prize-winner Clark Mollenhoff twice in the 1960s. During the decade, IADA ladies toured the new Merle Hay Plaza and enjoyed flower, decorating, and wig demonstrations. In 1965, they were taken to a showing of the Jack Lemmon film, *How to Murder Your Wife* at the state-of-the-art Capri Theatre at 42nd and University. As a sign of the times, 1964 convention-goers had a hootenanny. This was the decade IADA celebrated its golden jubilee convention.

Legislative

In two measures passed early by the 1961 legislature, tow-trucks were exempted from the requirements of the Iowa Commerce Commission, and the permissible time for paper plates was extended.

In April, 1964, Karl Jorde's annual report stated that Kahl and others "won our points one after another against, at times, terrific odds. Let us be thankful that we are not now operating under some of the oppressive and destructive legislation which was proposed."

In 1965, IADA fought a double tax on automobiles. The proposed legislation required collecting sales tax every time a used car was sold by a dealer. Kahl said during the battle, "To place a sales tax on the full selling price of used merchandise that has been taxed once and was traded in for other merchandise is double taxation, pure and simple." That year IADA also fought the nullification of Iowa's right-to-work law, endorsed a bill to license automobile manufacturers and their representatives, and supported a required drivers' education course for 16 and 17 year olds.

The 1969 session included passage of legislation requiring licensing for any company that leased vehicles, and for 72-hour "in-transit" stickers to permit out-of-state buyers to return home and dealers to bring cars into the state. As the 1969 session closed, Kahl wrote: "We can be thankful for a highly successful legislature with only the automobile franchise bill left for us to work for passage. Very few bills were defeated. Most of them are still in committees or on the calendars and can be acted on next year. Bills like those proposing staggered license renewal; state wage-hour law; permanent license plates; wheel taxes on cars; union shops; eliminating license refunds; etc. are all currently 'in the hopper' and could come out any time next year."

Getting Dealerships Together

In 1964, IADA members gathered in Grinnell for their first golf outing and dinner. This "swing-steak-stag" event became a traveling annual gathering hosted by local auto dealer groups. Both golfing and non-golfing dealers gathered for fellowship and a short business meeting after an afternoon of play. The second outing took place in Perry, the third in 1966 in Newton, and the fourth in Fort Dodge. In 1968, link-lovers played and dined in Marshalltown, and in 1969 they returned to Newton.

Fall District Meetings continued each year, with afternoon meetings changing in 1964 to start at 10 a.m. and adjourn by 4 p.m. for dealers, their office managers, and bookkeepers. A $2.50 registration fee covered lunch. While dealers addressed state legislative topics and national concerns, special educational opportunities and idea exchanges gave staff members opportunities to enhance their operational and administrative skills.

Following a "buzz session" at the 1962 meeting, Geraldine Lemaster of Danielson Motor Company wrote to Marjorie Grooms of the Crescent Motor Company of Ottumwa: "Preparation of the financial statement and balancing the ledger in one simplified operation did sound impossible compared to the usual month-end procedure. First thing yesterday morning I very dubiously started the statement without first balancing the ledger. The results were as you predicted—simplified, feasible and time-saving."

District meetings each fall gave dealers a chance to hear the latest issues impacting their businesses from staff and state officials. This photo is believed to be from the early 1960s.

Dealers had dealt with image and low-profit problems early in the 1960s, but at the 1966 dealer meetings they began discussing changes in the automotive world and the impact on their businesses: a wider range of models, options, engines, transmissions, interior trims, and gimmicks that would require larger inventories, more capital, and therefore more risk in automotive retailing. IADA promised to offer more service than ever before to assist dealers during these changing times.

Schukei Motor Company, Mason City, had a plastic horse in its showroom that attracted kids for picture-taking opportunities atop the steed. Ford dealer Clarence Schukei used it for his own photo opportunity with his sales staff in 1962.

The day after Thanksgiving in 1971, an IADA delegation departed Des Moines on a charter for Acapulco. A few of the individuals attending the IADA directors' meeting at the new Acapulco Princess included Hugh Hartley, Mrs. Tom Helms, Tom Helms, Mrs. Bonnie Hartley, Mrs. Norma Rose, Mrs. Les Weber, Les Weber, and Al Kahl.

the 1970s

"Today, more than at any time in the past, we must all become involved in the political arena for our own welfare. We must regularly converse with our state and federal lawmakers and law administrators so that they may understand our problems and be more sympathetic to our just causes. With the constantly increasing myriad of governmental controls being pressed upon us we cannot stand idly by hoping the trend toward socialism will be reversed by some magic means."

–Marvin Simpson, incoming IADA president, 1975, *IADA Directory*

In the '70s, dealers needed reason to celebrate their industry. Following one of their best years for sales and profitability in 1973, the auto industry spent much of the rest of the decade under attack for its perceived role in the energy crisis created by the Middle East oil embargo that began late in 1973. The association and its members dealt with the burden of "ever increasing governmental red tape," and with "consumer advocate devotees controlling both the Iowa Legislature and the U.S. Congress."

The Environment and Fuel Shortages

The '70s was the decade when most Americans learned the word "environmentalist." The first Earth Day was held in 1970. That same year, the 1970 Clean Air Act amendments addressed reduced lead in gasoline to control emissions and authorized the regulation of fuel

"If we want clean air it may be that we will have to restrict the number of cars per family. Drastic fuel shortages may also make this necessary. Larger metropolitan areas might have to limit the number of cars being driven, and also bar them from some parts of the city. Mass transportation systems will have to serve more people in the larger cities. ... The new car dealer who is in business now will have to be open-minded enough to keep up with changes in his own facilities, management and manpower needs if he wants to stay in business. The day of the guy who is in business for today only and won't attempt the necessary type of service and customer handling won't last. The manufacturers, for one, won't tolerate that type of attitude any longer."
—Tom Helms, IADA president, reprinted from the Davenport *Times Democrat* (April 8, 1973), second quarter, 1973, *Iowa Auto Dealer*

The association's officers in 1970 were Gary Lilly, president, Des Moines; Les Weber, first vice president, Dubuque; Ray Lauterbach, second vice president, Perry; Al Eisenmer, treasurer, Grinnell; and Marvin Hartwig, past president, Iowa City.

additives. But until the oil crisis, automobile gas efficiency was of little importance. Al Kahl, Gary Lilly, Lee Holt, Marv Harwig, Bill Perdock and Tom Helms traveled to Washington at the request of NADA to testify regarding the act.

In 1973, IADA president Tom Helms wrote, "If we want clean air it may be that we will have to restrict the number of cars per family. Drastic fuel shortage may also make this necessary....Perhaps some basic type of transportation, like a battery-powered car, or one with a rotary-type engine, will be used for the second auto the wife drives to do her shopping and such. We may be forced into this by sheer economic pressure. Many of the new ecological devices which must be installed on cars will be very expensive."

Car sales lagged. Later in the '70s, American automakers' efforts to produce fuel-efficient compact cars began to take shape. Smaller cars typically were made by foreign manufacturers and were not without safety concerns. In 1975, Iowa joined with other Midwestern states in working for a five-year moratorium on new federal mandates of safety and emission requirements. Their goal was to level off performance and operating costs of new vehicles. Iowans sent in more than 25,000 petition signatures to support the moratorium. In 1977, CAFE (corporate average fuel economy) standards were enacted, and a gas-guzzler tax passed in 1978.

At the end of the decade, when the Shah of Iran was exiled, a second oil crisis took place. IADA's 1979 president Bill Perdock wrote, "The public, through the consumerist, has expressed dissatisfaction toward our business. Our federal government has demanded safer, cleaner, more fuel-efficient vehicles. Yet, at the same time, our buying public has commanded the same transportation convenience and freedom that our business has provided for years. ...Changes in the use of energy will have a drastic effect on our business as we know it today. The use of gasoline, oil, electricity, and other energy sources has been cut back in recent years, and future required conservation is imminent."

Services

The early 1970s found IADA Services adding MasterCard and BankAmericard discount rates for auto dealers through Davenport Bank and Trust. IADA also began selling a number of products that met OSHA requirements, including shatter-proof light bulbs, safety blow guns, safety goggles, and exit lights.

As the programs of IADA continued to grow, so did the association's space needs. IADA moved to new office space—3,600-square-feet—in 1971 at 405 East First Street in Des Moines. The office added outgoing WATS (wide-area telephone service) lines and, at the end of the '70s, two incoming lines.

The IADA group insurance program was paying benefits at the rate of two-thirds of a million dollars a year at the beginning of the decade. IADA noted to members that at the 1970 rate, "it will take less than four years to provide benefits equal to those paid in the first 16 years of operation." Benefits continued to increase, with nearly $1 million paid out in 1971 and almost $1.25 million for the fiscal year that ended in June of 1973. In 1976, a loss in excess of $212,000 and huge increases in hospital and doctor costs forced rates to go up "considerably." The program by then covered some 5,000 dealers and employees.

A new G-W program appeared in November, 1970, having been rewritten to conform to state and federal laws and to apply to new-car buyers in addition to the used-car market. It provided a toll-free nationwide telephone number for holders to locate the nearest G-W dealer. Dealers had found that the new manufacturer warranties were reducing the time and the mileage for which such warranties applied, so the new G-W certificate permitted them to offer the same discount advantages on maintenance work that was available to buyers of used cars. Advisors from several states conferred on the certificate design, and eliminated the word "warranty." In 1976, national ads for the G-W Service Discount plan said it was "recognized in 34 states and Canada."

In 1975, IADA endorsed the creation of a dealer-owned credit insurance company and alerted dealers to get an agent qualified within the dealership to sell credit insurance no matter what credit program they used. Hawkeye Life Insurance Group became IADA's

"Our association takes on even more significance as we enter a period when the auto industry is apparently being cited as a major contributor to the energy crisis. I am sure that each of us is sympathetic with the problems facing our government in these critical times. However, it behooves our decision makers to remember the impact that the auto industry makes on the economy of this country. Major changes in the mode of personal transportation in the United States are undoubtedly necessary, but this change must be accomplished in a manner and on a time schedule that will cause the minimum disturbance to the consumer's desire to buy. He must not be encouraged to equate energy crisis to buying abstinence."
—H.E. Morrison, Jr., incoming IADA president, 1977, *IADA Directory*

The Ten DEMANDMENTS

Kemna Motor Company was founded as a GM dealership in Bancroft in 1956 by Joe Kemna. Doris Kemna worked with her husband "in between having children and once the older kids could baby sit." Joe died in 1995, and their son, Ken, took over. Doris continued to work at the dealership until January 1, 2007. She admits she still does a few things for Ken now and then. Doris provided IADA with "The Ten Demandments" that were included in the dealership's first employee handbook in 1977. The list was something the couple had seen and decided to reproduce.

1. **Don't lie.** It wastes my time and yours. I am sure to catch you in the end, and that is the wrong end.
2. **Watch your work, not the clock.** A long day's work makes a long day short; and a short day's work makes a long face.
3. **Give me more than I expect and I will give you more than you expect.** I can afford to increase your pay if you increase my profits.
4. **You owe so much to yourself that you cannot afford to owe anybody else.** Keep out of debt, or keep out of my place.
5. **Dishonesty is never an accident.** Good men, like good women, never see temptation when they meet it.
6. **Mind your own business, and in time, you will have your own business to mind.**
7. **Don't do anything here which hurts your self-respect.** An employee who is willing to steal for me is willing to steal from me.
8. **It is none of my business what you do at night.** But if dissipation affects what you do the next day and you do half as much as I demand, you will last half as long as you hoped.
9. **Don't tell me what I would like to hear, tell me what I ought to hear.** I don't want a valet to my vanity, but one for my money.
10. **Don't kick if I kick.** If you are worth correcting you are worth keeping. I don't waste time cutting specks out of rotten apples.

IADA officers in 1973 were Tom Helms, president; Mert Coover, first vice president; Ray Lauterbach, past president; and Marv Simpson, second vice president.

"After one of the best years in history (1973) both in units sold and net profits, the energy crisis jammed a wrench in the machinery and the automotive business slowed considerably; more so on the two coasts and in industrial areas. It is estimated by the automotive economists that between one thousand and two thousand retail outlets or dealerships will close before the end of 1974. We in the Midwest are in a more favorable position since food is very much in demand worldwide and will continue to be in demand as the population increases and shortages arise. Our state is the top food producer in the world. Automobile dealers have gone through some pretty lean years before, and the real pros are still running a profitable and rewarding agency."
—W.M. (Mert) Coover, incoming IADA president, 1974, *IADA Directory*

reinsurer and, following SEC approval, 223 IADA member dealers wrote credit insurance with Bankers United Life Assurance Company, a subsidiary of Life Investors. By April, 1978, the program passed $4.8 million in gross premium written. Before the end of the decade, more than $400,000 in premium was written in a single month.

At 1975 fall workshops, IADA announced an endorsed mechanical breakdown insurance program offered by Minnehomma Insurance Company. Premium written exceeded $1.3 million by April, 1978.

When state manual rates increased 10 percent in 1970 for workers' compensation insurance, IADA held fast to its rates, which started 30 percent below manual rates. The premiums paid by the IADA group averaged 37 percent below the authorized rates. As Les Weber

concluded his IADA presidency in 1972, he praised the association's program: "A dealer called in to inquire about the workers' compensation program. With the necessary information on employee classification and payroll, IADA was able to show that he could save $170 by entering the IADA group. His dues in the association are less than his savings on the workers' compensation group!" By that year, 330 dealers were participating, and while manual rates rose during the decade, IADA was able to keep starting rates at least 20 percent below manual rates. By 1976, 400 IADA members were enrolled.

With the merger of Computer Systems, Inc. and Automatic Data Processing, Inc. in 1972, IADA's ADP Dealer Data Processing, Inc. was formed as an "information-providing service." Employees at dealerships produced punched tapes, and the ADP center compiled information and processed reports to meet the specific needs of the dealership, including daily journals, detailed weekly schedules on parts and service accounts receivable, vehicle and financing accounts receivable, and other up-to-date records.

NADA had an AUTOCAP program with a dealer and consumer panel to mediate consumer complaints against auto dealers. The IADA staff began fielding consumer complaints in a "streamlined version" of that program for a trial period before deciding whether to appoint an action panel. In a cooperative agreement with the Des Moines Better Business Bureau and the State Consumer Protection Division, IADA dealers in central Iowa in November, 1979, announced a test program to handle consumer complaints.

In the 1970s, the association also found itself battling the Internal Revenue Service, which contested the tax status of IADA's insurance trust and workers' compensation program. The IRS conceded on the tax-exempt status of the association's group hospitalization program, but the workers' compensation program was forced to pay taxes on its investment income.

In 1972, only 11 of 975 eligible dealers didn't belong to the state association. By 1973, there were only six non-members. By 1976, IADA reported a membership of 819 within a difficult business environment.

Dealers Coming Together

Some 850 participants at the 1970 fall district meeting were treated to the theatrics of Gary Lilly as Charlie Fubar, auto dealer and owner of the FUBAR, Motor Co. As quickly as one of Fubar's endless troubles unfurled on stage, Al Kahl followed with possible solutions. Attendees heard recommendations for handling visits by sales tax auditors and federal wage and hour men, factory audits, odometer issues, and union leaders wanting to discuss contracts.

In 1972, the fall gatherings drew a crowd between 1,100 and 1,500 (accounts vary) to hear about new laws and how to comply with them. Dealerships learned about their responsibilities under automotive inspection regulations. County treasurers sent employees to consider how the new laws would affect title transfer. IADA introduced its Administrative Procedure Guide (APG) that year to detail the procedures every dealer needed to know about Iowa laws. This would become known as the first of the "Red Tape Update series." Fall meetings in 1973 were billed as "more Red Tape Update" with discussions on motor vehicle inspection, OSHA, titles, taxes, odometer tampering/mileage certification, and wage and hour regulations.

In 1974, IADA "decided that the time had come when the car and truck salesmen should have to accept some of the administrative responsibilities" and developed a salesmen's administrative procedures handbook that was introduced at the fall workshops. It "provided a clearer understanding of and compliance with the many restrictive laws and regulations." The cost of each book was 50 cents. IADA developed its own reference guide to OSHA and presented that information in 1975 to 815 workshop participants. More than 1,000 attended the 1976 meetings to learn about parts inventory control and management, OSHA, and the latest governmental regulations.

At the 1979 fall workshops, president Bill Perdock told dealers that 1980 would be the "most critical year of our time" because it was an election year. He labeled it "our last chance to stop, or at least slow up, the trend toward socialism, anti-business and bigger government." Perdock's advice to attending dealers: "Find out who the government and labor unions, the self-appointed consumer activists, and environmentalist groups are vigorously supporting, then support the other guy."

Throughout the decade, auto dealers continued to enjoy their golf outings around the state, bringing together approximately 90 golfers annually for a day of play, dinner, and an evening meeting, where they were joined by non-golfing dealers. In 1973, the first two-state golf challenge brought 113 dealers from Iowa and Illinois to Crow Valley Golf Club in Bettendorf, where they were joined by 22 more for a reception, dinner, and post-dinner activities.

Outstanding People

Clinton's Warren McEleney, who had never been president of IADA, assumed the presidency of NADA, with 250 Iowans—dealers and their wives—present for the national group's convention in Las Vegas in January, 1971. After his term of leading the 21,000-dealer group, McEleney was unanimously elected to another three-year term as the Iowa director for NADA. In 1975, McEleney chose not to run again, and Marvin Hartwig was elected to serve as Iowa's NADA director beginning in February, 1976.

"In the age of consumerism, business is the prime target of the do-gooders and we have twice as many shots being taken at us as ever before in history. Consequently it is imperative that we work harder as a team and keep in closer touch with our legislators and our staff. ... The past couple of years have been recession years in the auto industry and although our area probably wasn't hit as bad as some areas of the country it still has been quite lean for many. According to the economists we have turned the corner now and should be heading into a business upswing and new profit opportunities."
—W.M. (Mert) Coover, outgoing IADA president, 1975, *IADA Directory*

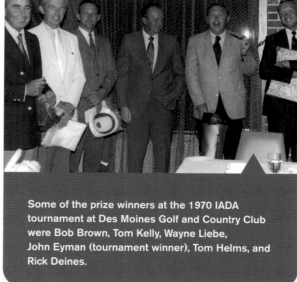

Some of the prize winners at the 1970 IADA tournament at Des Moines Golf and Country Club were Bob Brown, Tom Kelly, Wayne Liebe, John Eyman (tournament winner), Tom Helms, and Rick Deines.

In 1977, McEleney was honored as the national winner of the *Time Magazine* Quality Dealer Award. He was Iowa's only president of NADA and the state's first national recipient of the prestigious *Time Magazine* Award.

Marvin Hartwig, who had been the Iowa chairman of the Northwood Institute fund drive since 1969, was in 1972 named by Northwood Institute to receive the Dealer Education Award for Iowa. Hartwig's company won a judges' special citation in the 1972 Dealer Safety Awards Program sponsored by the Auto Dealers Traffic Safety Council of the Highway Users Federation of Safety and Mobility.

In 1972, the Iowa Automobile Young Timers sought to develop a group of men who were less than 35 years old and had "an eye on the future." With 28 members, Max Holmes, Jr., Des Moines, became president; Jim Getz, Newton, and Dean Lauterbach, Perry, were chosen as vice presidents; and Gary Kahn, Knoxville, was secretary/treasurer. They anticipated that other young men would join them in this arm of IADA, and Lauterbach was named to represent the young dealers on the IADA executive committee. In 1975, they had 31 members, and Gary Kahn became president. They hoped to double that number by appealing for more dealers to support the involvement of young men in their employment with management savvy and dreams, but little was written about their efforts after that time.

In the 1970s, IADA leaders unanimously added the following honorary members: Karl Jorde, Osage; Norman P. Dunlap, Ames; Robert Bickelhaupt, Clinton; Howard Howlett, Des Moines; and D.H. (Doc) Day, Clear Lake.

"We are fully aware of the recent erosion of respect and trustworthiness toward all business being brought about by governmental regulatory measures that will, if the trend is not checked, bring about the demise of our business as we know it today. You and I ask ourselves: 'What has caused this unreasoned antipathy toward business that is bringing about governmental involvement?' One of the more obvious reasons is the way the news media distorts the business picture. Scandals involving a handful of shady operators make headlines while the daily constructive and ethical activities of reputable businessmen—the vast majority—go unnoticed. The judgment of the general public tends to be formed on the basis of those sporadic incidents instead of the sustained performance of private business. ... We must communicate, collectively as IADA and individually as dealers, not only to the media, but to everyone concerned—our employees, our neighbors, our customers and our governmental officials. ... In my humble opinion, IADA's number one priority for the coming year is to aid and assist you in your responsibility to help put an end to this anti-business public attitude. We cannot sit by and 'let George do it.' Let's elect responsible congressmen and state legislators who are not anti-business."
—Wayne Johnson, incoming IADA president, 1976, *IADA Directory*

In 1979, at the January meeting of the state board, county directors, and NADA area chairmen, Kent Emery, the association' general counsel for nearly 20 years, was honored with a standing ovation and an engraved silver champagne bucket for his contribution to IADA.

In 1976, the association put together a committee to do a "long-range study of membership needs, future facilities and the operational functions of the organization." The seven dealers named to the group were Tom Helms, Warren McEleney, Marvin Hartwig, Lee Holt, Gary Lilly, Les Weber, and Bud Kahn.

Legislative

The most important legislation ever written by IADA was the "Dealer Bill of Rights," otherwise known as the Iowa Franchise Law. IADA legal counsel Kent Emery drafted the law and, in 1969, his associate Jim West began working with IADA on its passage.

The Iowa franchise law gave a dealer the right to sell his business or change management without factory approval, required the factory to prove the dealer's lack of qualification before canceling the franchise, and stated that new dealerships could not be arbitrarily established by the factory.

With the passage of the Auto Dealer Bill of Rights in the Iowa Legislature on March 12, 1970, IADA members felt like a huge weight—known as factory-imposed controls—was being lifted from their shoulders. This act was artfully written and based entirely on "public interest." The act was "created to insure the consumer that a dealer's service to the public would no longer be impaired by abusive franchise terms which are morally wrong and totally unfit."

Alfred Kahl, who celebrated 20 years with the IADA in 1970, was proud when the U.S. Supreme Court upheld the California Franchise Law, which had been patterned after Iowa's. He wrote: "It is now obvious that even the Supreme Court of the U.S. recognizes the tremendous power that the factories had over the franchisees and that court has validated once and for all the Iowa franchise law (along with 17 other states with similar laws) to balance off the inequities that exist between the power of the factory versus the dealer...This was a great victory for the franchised dealers of this nation." It was one of Kahl's proudest moments. "Don't ever forget it!" he emphasized.

In 1971, the IADA-backed measure to prohibit odometer tampering was adopted by the Iowa Legislature. Iowa's motor vehicle inspection law passed in 1972.

Kahl predicted that 1974 "would be the roughest session your association has ever encountered" with "Jim West, a member of your association counsel's firm, carrying the brunt of the legislative work." Kahl wrote: "The automobile has emerged as the ultimate symbol of energy abuse. That new laurel goes together with the auto being depicted as the villain of air pollution, the king of noise pollution, the mother of urban sprawl, and historically the cause of human sexual awareness in America."

Iowa's Uniform Commercial Credit Code (UCCC) received plenty of attention from West and others in 1974 to assure that the finance rates on motor vehicle sales were not affected. IADA also obtained a 30-day limitation to the complicated "holder-in-due-course" rule concerning the liability of lenders for vehicle defects. Later in the year, Jim West conducted clinics for hundred of dealers on how the UCCC applied to their businesses.

In 1961, Jim West, a young legal associate at the Nyemaster firm, began representing clients before the Iowa Legislature. Lobbyist West became the IADA's go-to guy in the 1970s. He was made an honorary member of IADA in 2004 in recognition of 35 years of representing IADA at the Iowa Legislature.

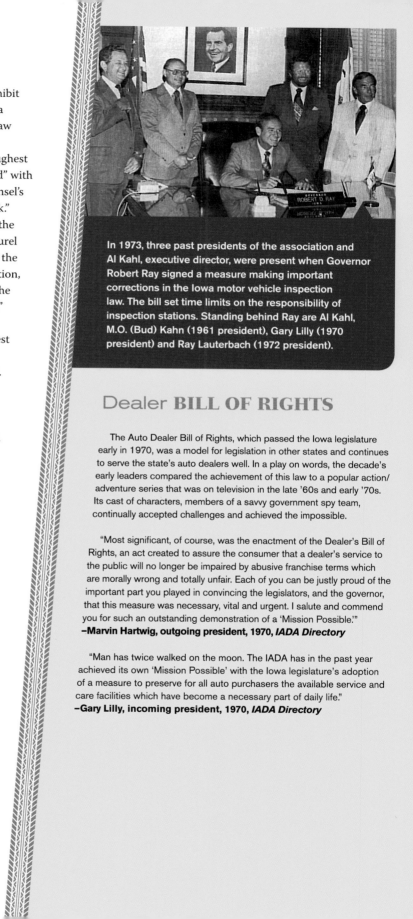

In 1973, three past presidents of the association and Al Kahl, executive director, were present when Governor Robert Ray signed a measure making important corrections in the Iowa motor vehicle inspection law. The bill set time limits on the responsibility of inspection stations. Standing behind Ray are Al Kahl, M.O. (Bud) Kahn (1961 president), Gary Lilly (1970 president) and Ray Lauterbach (1972 president).

Dealer BILL OF RIGHTS

The Auto Dealer Bill of Rights, which passed the Iowa legislature early in 1970, was a model for legislation in other states and continues to serve the state's auto dealers well. In a play on words, the decade's early leaders compared the achievement of this law to a popular action/adventure series that was on television in the late '60s and early '70s. Its cast of characters, members of a savvy government spy team, continually accepted challenges and achieved the impossible.

"Most significant, of course, was the enactment of the Dealer's Bill of Rights, an act created to assure the consumer that a dealer's service to the public will no longer be impaired by abusive franchise terms which are morally wrong and totally unfair. Each of you can be justly proud of the important part you played in convincing the legislators, and the governor, that this measure was necessary, vital and urgent. I salute and commend you for such an outstanding demonstration of a 'Mission Possible!'"
–**Marvin Hartwig, outgoing president, 1970, *IADA Directory***

"Man has twice walked on the moon. The IADA has in the past year achieved its own 'Mission Possible' with the Iowa legislature's adoption of a measure to preserve for all auto purchasers the available service and care facilities which have become a necessary part of daily life."
–**Gary Lilly, incoming president, 1970, *IADA Directory***

Much of the decade was spent protecting what rights dealers had and working to keep detrimental laws from becoming reality in Iowa. President Hank Morrison in 1978 summed up the association's greatest achievement of the year—and possibly the decade—as "our constant vigilance against undue government encroachments, either through legislation or regulations."

At the end of the decade, a major legislative issue concerned the legal difference between a van conversion and a motor home. The new law required van conversions to retain the identity of the original manufacturer. A 1969 law qualifying disclosure of minor transit damage gave IADA members hope by proving "that businesses can get legislative bodies to back off from some of the unrealistic, impractical and burdensome laws that were passed under the guise of being best for the consumer."

"Government bureaucrats are running rough shod over us and we take it with barely a whimper. Maybe it is because we are so used to being kicked around by our factory reps that we are calloused. ... Until we stick up for our rights and let ourselves be heard in the same way that the self-appointed consumer advocates so effectively achieve their ill conceived goals, we truly will become second class citizens quietly accepting their demands."
—Wayne Johnson, outgoing IADA president, 1977, *IADA Directory*

Summer board meeting attendees in 1974 included Les Weber, Wayne Johnson, Dewey Vukovich, Marv Simpson, Lee Holt, Mert Coover, Warren McEleney, Hank Morrison, and Marv Hartwig.

In the late '70s, IADA engaged a law firm specializing in OSHA laws for hearings on citations of two members regarding "ponderous, expensive, impractical explosion-proof lights" that were among the regulations. On April 17, 1979, IADA leaders learned they were successful in getting "some substantial relaxation in the enforcement of portable trouble light usage." Kahl wrote in "Flash Facts:" "We hope that EVERY member will see the value of paying their share to the IADA Legal Defense Fund next year. Lawyers cost money."

IADA Trips and Conventions

Throughout earlier decades, dealers and their spouses had enjoyed conventions with party themes featuring other cultures. In the 1970s, they started living out those cross-cultural experiences.

In November, 1971, an IADA group of 48 people combined a foreign excursion with a mid-winter conference. They were among the first occupants of the $43 million Acapulco Princess and met with dealers and dealer associations in Mexico.

In 1972, Miss America, Marilyn VanDerbur, appeared at the IADA gathering in Des Moines. In 1974, IADA held its convention in Hawaii. The association was set to take its convention to the new Hilton Inn in Des Moines for 1975, but the hotel wasn't completed in time, and they were welcomed to Tan-Tar-A at Lake of the Ozarks in April. More than 650 people and 39 exhibitors attended. The facility was labeled one of the best ever. Jesse Owens was the convention's wrap-up speaker.

IADA held its 1976 convention at Paradise Island in Nassau, Bahamas, in April. At this meeting, which was attended by 350, a bylaw change provided for a new board consisting of the five state officers, one director from each of the eight association districts, and three additional directors at large. The 1977 convention returned to the Hotel Ft. Des Moines, but with a post-convention trip to Guadalajara, Mexico. IADA went back to Tan-Tar-A in 1978, and in 1979 the association held its March gathering at the Diplomat Resort in Hollywood, Florida.

Theme Partiers
ENJOY THE WORLD

IADA conventions featured theme evenings linked to geography, such as a New Orleans party, a Monte Carlo night, and even hillbilly antics that created fun memories.

In 1978 Iowa hillbillies—like Hank Morrison and Tom and Joan Helms—were everywhere for the "Ozark Mountain Barbecue and Dance."

A carved ice sea horse and tropical flowers greeted 800 colorfully clad attendees at the 1970 luau buffet.

1970   **1971**   **1973**   **1978**

Putting together the IADA's annual conventions took a lot of dealer power. The 1971 convention committee, chaired by Dave Ostrem (left), included Bill Perdock, Jerry Howlett, Marv Simpson, Wayne Johnson, Ellie Elbert, Rudy Ulrick, and Duane Potts.

Costumes symbolic of the Far East and a small Japanese garden were part of the Oriental Interlude party.

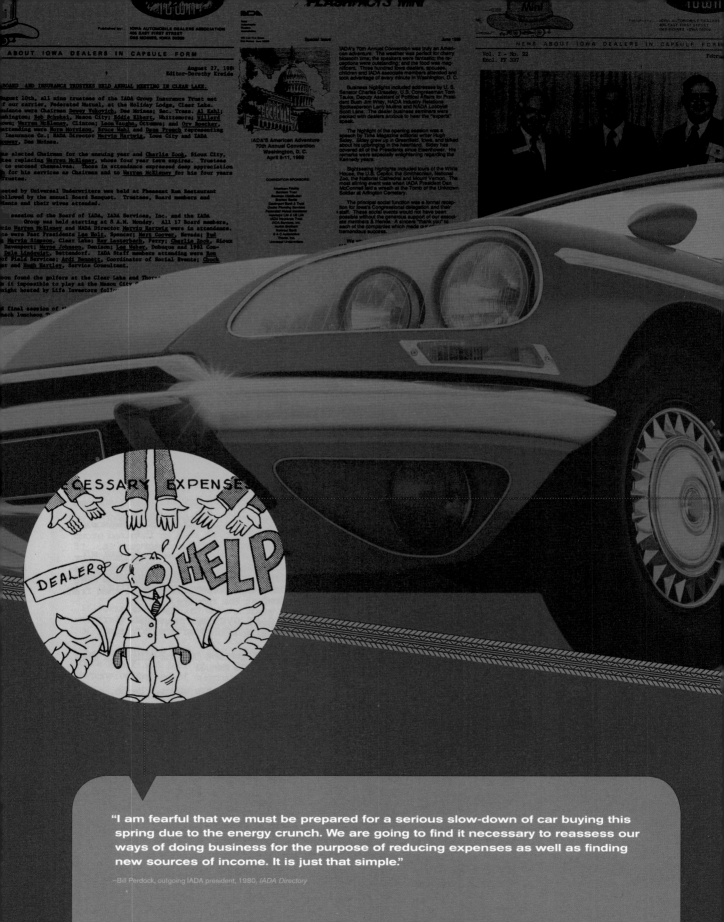

"I am fearful that we must be prepared for a serious slow-down of car buying this spring due to the energy crunch. We are going to find it necessary to reassess our ways of doing business for the purpose of reducing expenses as well as finding new sources of income. It is just that simple."

–Bill Perdock, outgoing IADA president, 1980, *IADA Directory*

the 1980s

"It is very easy to blame our problems on our government or the OPEC nations. Or should we say the grain embargo, or that our domestic manufacturers just didn't produce cars that people wanted to buy? Or that the imports have the only quality products with high gas mileage? How about inflation, high interest rates or out-of-sight new car sticker prices? Could it have been the Iran's capture of our embassy that took our people hostage and held them over 14 months? Or, maybe the heated presidential election that seemed to go on and on? Or is it that the consumer is just plain confused about price increase after price increase on cars that just aren't selling fast enough to keep our factories open? Or is it the rebates and free equipment offered by the manufacturer to entice the consumer to move into the market that confuses everyone? ... Used to be is gone. Our business is changing just like our cars are changing. Business conditions will improve and return but not as we once knew them. The form that our business will take is in its embryo state now. The exact form it will take is unknown by us, our manufacturer, or our consumers."

–Robert Schukei, president of IADA, 1980-81

As he left the IADA presidency in 1980, Bill Perdock said, "The cold realities of the '80s are that some of us will fail financially if we cannot, or will not, make adjustments to meet the changing times."

At the January, 1980, board meeting, president-elect Robert Schukei cited challenges that included the highest interest rates in history, the lowest customer interest in car products ever, gas availability, gas prices, inflation, recession, and possible war. "The burden placed upon the auto dealer today is the largest ever placed on dealers since the invention of the automobile," he said.

To stimulate lagging car sales, NADA launched a "buy now" media campaign to replace gas-guzzlers with efficient 1980 models, and IADA members were urged to get their local media involved. At the same time, IADA cautioned dealers not to take on "undesirable model cars the factories will push on you in order to get the smaller fuel-efficient models." Based on Iowa's dealer franchise law and the Federal "Good Faith Act," dealers were within the law to reject factory pressure and work toward "a better chance to survive this deep recession."

"In the 1980s, dealers, salesmen and sales managers must raise their sights to the $1,000 gross goal. It can't be done overnight or even next month but gradually it must come. We dealers must make upward adjustments in our gross goals during each price increase forced upon us by the manufacturer. Price increases are no more than the manufacturer covering his increased costs. ... For years dealers have been intimidated by their competitors and even their customers. Don't let this happen to you! Establish realistic gross levels; stick to them and increase them until you have your costs covered and then monitor them at every factory price increase. We know the domestic and even import manufacturers are changing their products to compete with the times. Don't you think it is time to change your methods as to how you sell them? I'm no sage, but I do know you can't lose a little on each sale and hope to make it up in volume."
—Robert Schukei, IADA president, "What's Going on Here?" column, July 16, 1980, *Iowa Auto Dealer "The Mini"*

In June, 1980, more than 100 dealers took part in IADA's Dealer Survival Kit seminars, geared to stimulate thinking toward profitable times ahead. Dealers were desperate to identify the ways and means to control expenses, increase parts and service income, and develop new merchandising techniques. To help them find dollars for their businesses, "Flash Facts" began carrying information on applying for SBA loans, plus tips on getting back to basics for office managers and department managers of new cars, used cars, service, body, and parts. But by mid-year, IADA estimated that 60 Iowa franchised dealers had gone out of business. In 1981, IADA president Eddie Elbert said, "During 1980 we lost 10 percent of our Iowa dealers. In part they were forced out of business because of financial failures, lack of sales, high interest rates and just plain business pressures. The bleak picture is that we will probably lose more. For the survivors it will continue to be a challenge."

The association focused on turning business around for its members, and the 1980 fall district meetings were billed as "Revival Workshops." The decade was off to a rough start. By 1985, IADA had 679 franchise dealer members, down from more than 850 when the decade began. Some 580 dealers were members in 1988.

Changes

In 1981, IADA held a ceremonial "burning of the mortgage" just 18 months after payments on its building at East First and Locust began. The majority of space in this downtown Des Moines building was leased to a renter through January of 1984.

In October, 1989, staff members packed their belongings, as IADA's building was to be torn down to make way for a parking lot. IADA moved to a new

This 'N THAT

"Alfred A. Bruesewitz, owner of Bruesewitz Chevrolet, remembers '33 when times were really bad. He has sold cars from the same location for 60 years and remembers 1933 during the Great Depression, when he sold just two cars all year. 'But we got by,' he adds. 'The current recession doesn't match those times. God, no, people would kill themselves if that happened again!' A native of Grafton, he turned 82 in June and continues to turn in 60-hour work weeks."
–This 'N That column, July 16, 1980,
Iowa Auto Dealer "The Mini"

"William Hoffman is still driving and still working as a bookkeeper at the Hudgins Ford dealership in Radcliffe. This may sound like a routine thing for most of us, however, he recently celebrated his 100th birthday. He began work at the Ford dealership at age 71 and has been adding, subtracting, multiplying and dividing ever since. He was honored at an open house in Radcliffe."
–This 'N That column, March, 1988,
Flash Facts Mini

office building at 1111 Office Park Road in West Des Moines that offered a more functional and spacious work environment, including a boardroom for meetings by dealer groups.

After 30 years at the helm of IADA, Alfred Kahl left office on October 1, 1981, turning daily operational responsibilities and the title of executive vice president over to Gary W. Thomas, IADA's then general manager. In retirement, Kahl worked on a "Flash Facts" index and an updated Administrative Procedures Guide.

In 1983, Thomas became one of only 91 individuals in the country who, that year, earned the coveted Certified Association Executive (CAE) designation. The CAE credential recognized his demonstrated skills and leadership in the association management arena. Thomas was a founding member of Iowa Traffic Safety Now and received its 1987 Distinguished Service Award for his commitment to safety belt education and use.

A sleek logo was introduced in 1983 (top) and replaced by today's logo in 1989 (below).

IADA unveiled a new corporate logo in 1983. It was described as "more refined" with "tastefully bold simplicity." Like the automobile of the '80s, it had more "refined, sleek lines." The logo changed again in 1989 when a forward slant was given to the letters of the acronym. A crossbar that resembled a roadway ran across the letters.

Public Image

Dealers have always been concerned with their public image. But with the decade's rough start, Thomas and his team made an all-out effort to help dealers look good by doing good.

In partnership with the Des Moines Better Business Bureau and the Iowa Attorney General's Office, IADA continued its efforts to address consumer complaints against dealers. The association worked to identify a "key man" at each dealership who would handle that company's consumer complaints. In 1983, IADA launched AUTOCAP, a statewide automotive consumer action program, to address complaints that could not be resolved between a dealer and customer. They established a third-party panel to handle cases requiring mediation. Auto dealer panel members included dealers David Wright (Carlisle), Dave Ostrem (Des Moines), Theresa Kingma (Pella), and Bob Jensen (Marshalltown). Complaints

Three of the 1980 officers were Eddie Elbert, first vice president; Robert Schukei, president; and Willard Loots, second vice president. Not pictured were H.E. (Hank) Morrison, treasurer, and Bill Perdock, past president.

against auto dealers in the 1980s were quickly cut in half and dropped from the number one problem to sixth on the Attorney General's complaint list. Most cases were simply handled by the association's AUTOCAP staff.

Of the drop in complaints, IADA president Bob Axtell said in 1983, "What makes this especially interesting is the fact that sales in Iowa are up as high as 18 to 20 percent. Yet this higher volume is yielding fewer complaints." AUTOCAP was described to dealers as "your program to keep consumers out of government channels" that "strives to keep your customers satisfied." The national average for case duration was 53 days, but IADA kept its average resolution time to 30 days. By 1985, some 95 percent of Iowa's franchised dealers were participating in the program, and of the nearly 200 program inquiries, only 11 cases had gone to mediation.

The focus on safety and accident prevention continued as auto dealers worked to get public education materials into communities. In 1982, IADA gave 13 copies of a slide show, "One Drink Too Many," produced by the Highway Users Federation, to the Iowa Department of Public Safety for use with service clubs. IADA was involved in a December proclamation for Drunk Driving Awareness Week, and the next year sponsored a statewide campaign, "Not Sober? Pull Over."

In 1983, a slide show/filmstrip from the National Dealer Safety and Mobility Council was loaned by Iowa dealerships to local civic groups. It was called "Double Trouble: Drugs and Driving." President Bob Axtell wrote, "The trend of thought toward drunk driving is changing from one of indifference to one of outrage and intolerance. Let's help propel this change."

Also in 1983, IADA began promoting the greater use of child safety seats. The program, "For Your Child's Sake… Use a Little Restraint," included billboards, public service announcements, and posters and brochures available at dealerships. U.S. Secretary of Transportation Elizabeth Dole and Iowa's new governor, Terry Branstad, were on hand for the program's kickoff. IADA provided more than 100 child safety seats to dealers for use with DOT's county loan programs that year. The campaign—which received more than five million column inches of press and numerous broadcast segments—helped persuade the Iowa legislature to pass car seat legislation in 1986.

In 1985, IADA donated $500 to the NADA Charitable Foundation for the purchase of practice mannequins for CPR training. At least five such mannequins would be presented by IADA and NADA to Iowa Red Cross Chapters during the rest of the decade.

In 1986, IADA and the Iowa Motor Truck Association jointly gave $20,000 to the Department of Public Safety to fund new digital telecommunications hardware to help replace the state's obsolete winter road condition phone service.

Throughout the decade, the message was sent again and again to Iowans: new car dealers care.

"As I see down the road, credit could possibly take on a new form for small business in 1981, especially the auto dealer. Credit, or shall we call it accounts receivable, is getting a lot of visibility these days. Interest rates reaching about 20 percent—and would you believe all dealers who have floor plan costs are in fact borrowing money for their accounts receivable? In reality, accounts receivable money that we dealers carry could be used to relieve floor plan interest if we didn't have accounts receivable. … If your customer gets interest on his money on a daily basis in his checking account and he knows he will have to pay interest from day one using his plastic bank card, doesn't it make sense for him to use YOUR accounts receivable for free if you let him? Even if you charge him a finance charge on over 30 days you are the loser—you simply cannot charge your customer enough to cover what your floor plan costs are. Money is expensive today and tomorrow who knows—maybe more or maybe less, but be assured your customer will look to you as a small business owner and say 'charge it.'"
—Robert Schukei, IADA president, "What's Going on Here?" column, May, 1980, *Iowa Auto Dealer "The Mini"*

Services

In 1981, IADA offered three new services. It began offering low-cost printing on business cards through a Minnesota printing firm. It formed an alumni club that allowed former dealers to participate in association events for only $25 per year. And it endorsed Unicover III, a new property-casualty insurance concept from Universal Underwriters.

Refunds to dealers participating in the association's programs totaled nearly $1 million in 1983, with workers' compensation reaching $468,535, group health/life and disability returning $463,259, and the Hawkeye Credit Life program totaling $25,000 in refunds.

In 1984, IADA added disability insurance through the American Fidelity Assurance Co. of Oklahoma. That year the creation of a finance and insurance (F&I) computer program, with software that included leasing, got underway at IADA. By the next year, 20 franchised dealers were using the software on IBM PC or PCjr hardware. That program, overhauled to make it more user-friendly, expanded to 70 dealers by 1988.

Insurance costs soared during the decade, but increases were typically followed by refunds. In 1985, Federated Insurance returned more than $2.3 million to more than 70 percent of member dealers participating in group health and life programs. In 1987, two refunds for workers' compensation participants were presented, followed by a third in 1989. In 1987, 78 percent of IADA's 580 dealer members utilized the association's health insurance plan, and 65 percent used its workers' compensation program. Health insurance premiums continued to rise as the decade closed, and IADA's Insurance Trust moved to age-rated insurance premiums.

At the end of the decade, Hawkeye Life, which had existed for 13 years to sell life and health insurance, had more than $10 million in assets. The company was the largest producer of life, accident, and health insurance for auto loans in Iowa. Some 170 dealers were participating in the program.

IADA continued to respond to dealer needs with programs and services. To help dealers meet the requirement of Iowa's Right-to-Know law, IADA developed Right-to-Know program manuals and video cassettes and held workshops in 1986, 1987, and 1989 for dealerships. When the Attorney General's office began focusing on dealer advertising practices in 1986, IADA began sponsoring advertising practices workshops. During the decade IADA also promoted insurance licensing, sales, successorship, and parts/inventory management seminars.

As the decade closed, IADA introduced Sprint Long Distance service to dealerships.

Taking a Stand

In 1980, ICAR (Iowa Committee of Automotive Retailers, a political action committee) contributed $8,000 to 82 candidates in Iowa, and 62 were victorious. Some 20 percent of Iowa dealers contributed to the PAC. With the fall election of 1982, IADA members got behind NADA's DEAC (Dealer Election Action Committee) and further developed ICAR with a "Fair Share" campaign. Dealers' political involvement grew. They traveled to the nation's capitol each fall for NADA's Washington Conference. There they were briefed on key auto dealer concerns and visited members of Iowa's congressional delegation. IADA members exceeded their 1984 DEAC goal by 7 percent, making the association one of only 11 state organizations recognized nationally for its performance. In 1987, some 281 dealers contributed to meet campaign goals of $30,000, and the IADA goal was met again in 1988 for DEAC. By 1989, the DEAC/ICAR goal reached $50,000.

Legislative

In 1980, IADA said it was proud that "no laws detrimental to auto dealers" passed. Allowable finance rates on new models rose from 15 to 18 percent. In the 1980s, IADA fought attempts to increase license fees and use taxes, additional mandatory employer-provided benefits, and any change that would make it easier for van converters to operate in Iowa. They worked for staggered vehicle registrations based on purchase dates. IADA lobbied for mandatory seat belt and child restraint legislation (passed in 1986), to allow seven days to title an out-of-state vehicle (up from two days), and to increase speed limits on four-lane divided highways to 65 mph.

In 1981, IADA proposed modifications to DOT inspection law and enforcement procedures. In February of 1984, dealers Dan McConnell (Waterloo) and Stew Hansen (Des Moines) presented IADA's concerns to the

Bob Schukei and Charles Grassley, one of Iowa's congressmen in the House of Representatives, in 1980.

Present in 1986 for the signing of the fleet subsidy bill by Governor Branstad were Martha Martell, George White, Bob Schukei, Hank Morrison, Orv Roecker, Dave Ostrem, Eddie Elbert, Marv Hartwig, Lee Holt, Chuck Yoder, Bob Campbell, Ron Nanke, and Gary Thomas. The bill was repealed one year later.

Iowa Transportation Commission in a call for "a strict, effectively enforced inspection program that is workable and successful in ensuring safer vehicles on the roads." They called the current program "intolerable." They asked that 18 non-essential items be deleted, and that roadside spot checks take place. Eventually, the state repealed the inspection law.

The biggest national dealer problem in 1986 was that manufacturers were selling vehicles to rental company fleets at prices lower than dealers could get. As an added blow, the rental companies then sold the used units for lower prices than dealers could afford. At that time several of the big rental companies were actually owned by motor vehicle manufacturers, so they were giving preference to their own companies to the detriment of dealers.

NADA determined that the solution would have to be handled on a state-by-state basis. Iowa was the first and only state to attack this problem head-on. In 1986, landmark anti-fleet subsidy legislation passed with incredible effort from Jim West and hundreds of dealers who mobilized to do battle. "Unfortunately, there were some bitter arguments

among members because not all agreed with IADA's plan," said then legal counsel Martha Martell.

The victory was sweet and short-lived. GM had a low interest rate program that the company advertised as "not available in Iowa." The factory used the anti-fleet legislation as an excuse, and IADA sued. Non-rental fleet business that once belonged to Iowa dealers was given to dealers in neighboring states.

The retaliation was too much. In 1987, IADA went back to the Iowa legislature and repealed the law. As IADA lobbyist Jim West said, "We were spitting crow feathers" for years.

By the end of the decade Iowa legislators were challenged by "the lack of revenue to move projects and ideas forward." IADA was concerned with defending current title branding priorities, resisting amendments proposed by van converters, defending the Sunday closing law, defending the existing lemon law, and supporting the creation of a state underground storage tank insurance pool.

"Imagine, for a 'fleeting' moment if you will, the tremors that would be felt if 25 percent of all new car sales in the country were suddenly stripped from the hands of franchised dealers. Or even 50 percent. On top of that, imagine the remaining units that dealers are selling suddenly increased in price by $200 to $300 per unit. ... These conditions aren't imaginary. ... Fleet subsidies given by manufacturers to fleet and leasing companies which buy their cars directly are helping those companies compete head on with franchised dealers in the new and used car markets. In fact, dealers can hardly compete at all because fleet companies can sell current model year units to the consuming public more cheaply than dealers can buy them—in many cases $600 to $800 less than dealer cost!"
—John O. Falb, IADA president, August 8, 1984, *Flash Facts*

When dealers talk about favorite IADA memories, the topics reach beyond the achievements of the association. Many times they revolve around conventions, traveling, friendships, and informal get-togethers that included their wives. This 1982 group included (Row 1) John and Sally Falb, Mert and Lena Coover, Dorthea Holt, Ellen Perdock, Marge Kahl, Ray and Betty Lauterbach, Bill Perdock, Al Kahl, and Leon Vaughn. First step (Row 2) Bob Axtell, Lee Holt, and Joan Helms. Second step (Row 3) Dick and Helen Dirks, Tom Helms, and Mary Elbert. Top row: Orv Roecker, Marv Hartwig, Lee Roecker, Verna Hartwig, Eddie Elbert, Margaret Johnson, and Wayne Johnson.

Gatherings

IADA's annual conventions took dealers to Kuilima, Hawaii, in 1980, Tan-Tar-A in 1983 and 1987, and Orlando in 1985. The association's pre- or post-convention trips were to Mazatlan, Mexico, in 1981, Austria in 1982, and Brazil in 1984. The 1982 event at the Des Moines Marriott included a roast of Alfred Kahl, with his wife Marge and children Kandi and John present.

Just under 300 individuals attended IADA's 1989 convention in Washington, D.C. Events included tours of the White House, Smithsonian, Kennedy Center, Library of Congress, and Mount Vernon. Outgoing IADA president Dan McConnell laid a wreath at the Tomb of the Unknown Soldier. There was a dinner cruise on the Potomac and a visit to the newest monument at the time, the Vietnam Memorial.

Des Moines conventions found dealers and their spouses dancing to the Rumbles as well as sock hopping at Jukebox Saturday night on Court Avenue, enjoying a "chocolate affair" and fireworks, and watching IADA president Leon Vaughn be sawed in half by a magician. The spouses visited Terrace Hill, historic Valley Junction, the new Plaza Condominiums, and Salisbury House.

Golf

IADA's golf enthusiasts kicked off the decade with two multi-state gatherings in June, 1980. The first was at Galena's Eagle Ridge Resort for dealers from Wisconsin, Illinois, and Iowa. A week later, a second one was held at the Sioux City Boat Club's new course for dealers in western Iowa, eastern Nebraska, and South Dakota.

The following year IADA began to talk sports at post-golf dinners. During the decade, speakers included former Iowa and Kansas City Chiefs' star Ed Podalak, NFL official John Keck, ISU basketball coach Johnny Orr, University of Iowa basketball coach Tom Davis and athletic director Bump Elliott, UNI basketball coach Eldon Miller, and Cedar Rapids Gazette sports columnist Gus Schrader. IADA golfers played at Wakonda (Des Moines), Elmwood (Marshalltown), Des Moines Golf and Country Club, Oakland Acres (Grinnell), Lake Panorama (Panora) and Sunnyside Country Club (Waterloo).

Howard Sole, 88-year-old past president of IADA, provided the 1981 golf highlight by having the low score in a foursome that included Bill Perdock, Charlie Zook, and Al Kahl.

Dealer Meetings

In the 1980s, IADA sometimes added a statewide "blitz" to its meeting schedule to reach dealers in as many as 24 locations with critical information during a short period of time. Dealer fall meetings explained such topics as IRS tax rulings, debt collection and repossession, hazardous waste, the lemon law, repeal of state inspection law and red title laws, odometer fraud, Right-to-Know law, and the title branding law. IADA also presented information about DEAC/ICAR, a new health insurance retiree program, and the introduction of IADA's Forms Management System for dealers.

"The small businessman today is fed up with policy, inflation, high interest rates and government regulations that literally are holding our feet to the fire. It's time we, in small businesses, raise our voice and use our strength to let the government know our position on every issue affecting business and jobs."
—Robert Schukei, incoming IADA president, 1980, *IADA Directory*

1980 Board members present for their official photo were (Row 1) Don Hindmarsh, John Falb, Jr., Bill Perdock, Bob Schukei (president), Eddie Elbert, Willard Loots, and Warren McEleney; (Row 2) Steve Clarke, Don McGurk, Robert Axtell, Leo Levien, Chet Danielson, Dick Witham, Clair Conway, Dick Dirks, and Marv Hartwig.

Employee issues gained attention. Hiring and firing rights and responsibilities, unemployment regulations, employee testing (drug, alcohol, polygraph), workers' compensation claims, and sexual harassment issues were part of such programs in the 1980s.

The 1983 meeting, which dealt entirely with the topic of staggered auto registrations, drew 1,000 people, representing 60 percent of Iowa's dealerships, to do "practical exercises to exhibit the problems of staggered registrations."

People

In 1981, Marvin Hartwig was re-elected NADA director for Iowa. He served as secretary, vice president for NADA Region III, and in 1986 became NADA treasurer, serving two terms in that post. In 12 years as an NADA leader, Hartwig also was part of that group's charitable foundation, convention committee, industry relations committee, and finance committee. In 1988, the year Eddie Elbert replaced Hartwig as Iowa's NADA director, Hartwig became Iowa's first member of DEAC's President's Club with a $5,000 contribution, saying, "We need our second DEAC President's Club member from Iowa."

Warren McEleney won the 1982 AIADA-Sports Illustrated Dealer of Distinction Award, one of the most prestigious awards presented to automobile dealers by the American International Automobile Dealers Association. In 1985, he received the Distinguished Service Citation from the Automotive Hall of Fame in Midland, Michigan. At that time he was involved with three dealerships representing 11 line makes.

In 1986, past president John Falb, West Union, was one of only ten dealers in the nation to participate in NADA's Project 2000, a blue-ribbon panel of dealers looking at changes in the franchise system.

Added during the 1980s to IADA's impressive roster of honorary members were M.O. "Bud" Kahn, Clear Lake; Marvin Simpson, Waterloo; Floyd Hughes, Sr. and Floyd Hughes, Jr., Council Bluffs; Dwight Burkhart, Independence; Chuck Sinclair, Mason City; Wayne Johnson, Denison; Kent Emery, retired IADA legal counsel and writer of the heralded dealer franchise law; Ray Lauterbach, Perry; Gary Lilly, West Des Moines; William Cramblit, Jr., Ottumwa; Marvin Hartwig, Iowa City, State Senator Lee Holt, Spencer; and Alfred Kahl, Des Moines.

In 1984, IADA established a Half Century Hall of Fame to honor dealerships that had been in business for 50 years or more and existed continuously under the ownership of the same family. Twenty-five charter members were inducted at the 1984 convention, and 25 others qualified for induction.

Brighter Outlook

A market opinion research survey indicated in 1981 that 16.7 million people were ready to buy new cars "under the right conditions." Total auto sales had increased every year since 1980, when sales and dealership profits bottomed out. By 1985 the average Iowa dealership was selling $2.8 million in products and services. Dealerships employed nearly five percent of the state's population and auto sales made up 13.5 percent of all retail sales.

IADA decided the "right conditions" existed for an auto show and set up "FUTURESHOW" for November 13–17, 1985, at the Des Moines Convention Center. As the first new automobile exhibit in 30 years, FUTURESHOW displayed more than $2 million of new and concept cars and trucks—a total of 130 vehicles—to nearly 37,000 Iowa consumers with the support of sponsoring dealers and participating Hy-Vee stores around the state. The winner of the grand prize drawing received $10,000 toward the purchase of a new car. She chose a 1986 Pontiac 6000 STE from Ramsey Pontiac in Des Moines. In November of the following year, more than 70 Iowa automobile dealerships sponsored an AUTO-XPO themed "Unveiling Tomorrow's Classics." It displayed more than 120 vehicles for 1987 to some 32,600 people who attended a five-day show at the Des Moines Convention Center. Antique automobiles also were featured.

"Recent figures show that the average franchised new car dealership in the United States experienced a 9.3 percent increase in total dealership sales in 1982 compared to 1981. Total sales have increased each year since 1980, when sales and dealership profits bottomed out. Total U.S. dealership sales also increased five percent, from $136.6 billion to $143.9 billion. In Iowa, dealership sales reached $1.77 billion, with the average dealership selling $2.8 million in products and services. Our sales make up 13.5 percent of all retail sales in the state. Iowa dealerships employ nearly five percent of all retail employees in the state. ... Massive capital investment by manufacturers to rebuild and refurbish assembly plants is beginning to show strong results. Dealer showrooms are displaying exciting new products such as we've never seen: new classes of automobiles that create strong appeal to new car buyers. Light and medium duty truck sales are booming. Larger luxury cars are becoming a popular choice again. New designs, new engineering features are constantly unfolding."
—John O. Falb, IADA president, 1985, *IADA Directory*

FUTURESHOW

DES MOINES   1985

FUTURESHOW, Iowa's first auto show in three decades, brought 36,865 car buffs, car shoppers and curious spectators to the five-day downtown Des Moines extravaganza.

Happy NEW YEAR

From IADA Board of Directors & Staff

The number of automobile dealers across the nation was growing smaller.
The IADA looked for ways to keep the remaining dealerships solid and profitable
and the industry strong in Iowa and throughout the country.

the 1990s

"There have been few times in history when automobile dealers have been confronted with such confusing changes in the way that we must conduct business. These changes are presented by the manufacturers who are striving for economies and efficiencies as well as the growing presence of chains. We all are watching carefully and wondering what effect these changes will have on our own dealerships. The need for effective association leadership has never been greater."

–**John O. Falb,** NADA Director, January 23, 1998, *Action Update*

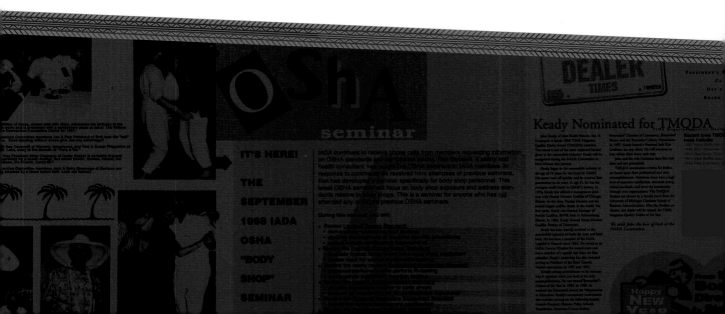

IAD Foundation
MAKES A DIFFERENCE

"The mission statement of the IAD Foundation for Education clearly identifies the correlation between education and industry. The actions that the Foundation has taken validate its commitment to the automotive service industry future. Both the students and the program at North Iowa Area Community College have been beneficiaries of the Foundation's actions.

Many of the IAD Foundation scholarship students who have graduated from the automotive service technology program are gainfully employed at area dealerships. The Foundation also has provided financial assistance to the community college automotive programs for several years.

Additionally, the IADA pioneered a unique partnership with and among Iowa automotive community college instructors by hosting an annual workshop where an open discussion of educational and service industry strengths and concerns are brainstormed and solutions and ideas are shared. This helps to make program and curriculum changes/improvements that benefit all concerned. NIACC is grateful for the generosity and assistance of Iowa's automotive dealers and proud to be associated with such a fine, pro-active organization."
–Greg Arrowood, Instructor, Automotive Technology, North Iowa Area Community College, Mason City, August, 2007

Ryan Brooks (third from left) was the 1999 Bob Brown Scholarship winner. Pictured are Mike Kossack, Bill Cox, Brooks and Ron Brown of the Des Moines Chevrolet dealership.

In 1989, there were 520 new car and truck dealers in Iowa. By 1999, there were only 443. The strong were focused and surviving, ensuring industry integrity through knowledgeable, well-trained people.

In 1995, IADA established the IAD Charitable Foundation (for Education), a non-profit entity with its own board and goal of assisting youth in their educational pursuit of automotive industry careers. The foundation began as the vision of George White, George White Chevrolet in Ames, who interested two colleagues in the idea: Harry McMullen, McMullen Ford, Council Bluffs; and Charlie Zook, Charlie Zook Motors of Sioux City. White died in 1995, and the foundation was inactive for two years. McMullen began recruiting more foundation board members to commit to a $10,000 contribution—$2,000 per year—for the presentation of scholarships. By 1998, McMullen, Zook, and nine other members were on board. Seven scholarships were presented in1998 to Iowa high school seniors. By 1999, there were 13 founding members of the foundation, and 10 more scholarships were given out. Late that year Glenda Millard, Mid-States Ford, Des Moines, became a member with a $10,000 contribution in memory of her husband, Dick Millard.

George White, George White Chevrolet of Ames, conceived the idea of an educational foundation that would award scholarships to students who wanted a career in the automotive industry.

DEAC/ICAR

IADA closed its 1990 fundraising year for DEAC/ICAR just shy of a $50,000 goal, with 215 dealers contributing. In 1992, when a team approach was used to generate PAC funds, eight teams were designated, one for each of the IADA districts. Some 35 percent of dealers participated in raising $36,000 by November. The $50,000 statewide goal wasn't met in 1995 but was exceeded in 1996 when 231 dealers contributed $55,845. In 1999, IADA members contributed more than $26,000 to DEAC and more than $50,000 to ICAR.

Iowa's sustaining members of the DEAC President's Club in the early 1990s were Marv Hartwig and Warren McEleney. In 1995, Pete Pohlman, Lujack-Schierbrock, joined the President's Club with his leadership gift. John Deery, Sr., Deery Brothers Automotive Group, made his commitment in 1999.

Educational Efforts

IADA continued to reach dealers through workshops on a variety of topics during the 1990s. More than 1,600 people took part in 11 title workshops with IDOT to learn about changes resulting from the Truth in Mileage Act of 1986 and of new forms put into place in the state beginning July, 1990.

Right-to-Know workshops detailing employee safety and compliance with OSHA dominated the decade. Dealer representatives took part in Ken Strosahl's "train the trainer" sessions so they could return and teach other employees about the proper handling of hazardous chemicals in the workplace. Their efforts were timely, as OSHA inspectors began sweeping the state in 1997 looking for non-compliant dealerships. Other special workshops during the decade focused on dealer management, insurance issues, and the media and confrontation for dealer principals.

Fall meeting topics in the 1990s addressed a diverse and ever-increasing list of state and federal issues, in addition to providing updates about NADA and IADA programs, services, and legislative concerns. Information was shared on D-plate options, IDOT enforcement audits and investigations, vehicle registrations, collection of overdue accounts, lease disclosure, advertising, and new title and secure power of attorney forms. In addition to OSHA compliance, the fall meetings addressed federal wage and hour laws, consumer credit, compliance with the Americans with Disabilities Act, cash reporting laws, tips for avoiding discrimination claims, luxury taxes, administration of the Federal Excise Tax for truck drivers, and retrofitting air bag on-off switches. Unfair competition was the dealer hot topic as the decade ended.

Dealers continued to go to Washington, D.C., each fall to learn about federal legislation and meet with the state's congressional representatives on such issues as health insurance costs, multiple employer welfare arrangements (similar to the IADA health insurance trust), multi-purpose vehicle fees, mandatory binding arbitration, title branding legislation, teen employee driving, and stolen auto parts.

Coming Together for Convention and Football

A highlight of the 1990 IADA convention was an idea exchange. Every dealer had three minutes to share his idea for making additional profits or cutting expenses in the dealership. A vote by those present that year put $250 in the pocket of Rusty Jones, J.M. Jones and Sons, Inc., Manchester. The idea? Jones presented a report card at the end of each month to all the lending institutions his dealership worked with, sharing the number of cars sold, the number financed, and how many the particular lending institution financed. His report card enabled Jones to get more cars financed through some of the lending institutions. Subsequent winners were Don Pierson of Don Pierson Ford, Spencer, in 1991, and Craig Delzell, Delzell Motor Company, Burlington, in 1992.

Iowa dealers joined with dealers from Kansas for a 1991 convention in San Antonio, and they met in the Ozarks at Tan-Tar-A in 1993. Basketball coaches and conference competitors Johnny Orr of Iowa State and

In 1997, IADA began sponsoring annual dealer gatherings on football Saturdays when the University of Iowa and Iowa State University played each other. Iowa congressional representative Jim Ross Lightfoot and Dean Beecher are shown at one gathering.

Roy Williams of Kansas made a joint presentation at the Tan-Tar-A gathering. Attendance at out-of-state and other destination conventions had been dropping, in part because dealers were offered many special travel opportunities by auto manufacturers. In 1995, IADA held its annual meeting in the spring, but without added convention attractions. The association's breakfast for Iowa dealers and spouses at the NADA convention early each year became IADA's biggest member participation event. In March, 1998, a few IADA members joined auto dealers from Kansas, Nebraska, Colorado, South Dakota, and Wyoming in Maui for a multi-state convention.

Beginning in 1997, IADA offered dealers an opportunity to purchase tickets for the University of Iowa versus Iowa State University football rivalry. IADA's pre-game tent party in Ames with barbecue was a sell-out that year, as it was in Iowa City the next year and Ames again in 1999. This successful game day event—which drew between 300 and 400-plus participants—was held through 2003.

Golf

The summer golf outing tradition continued throughout the '90s at Finkbine in Iowa City, Elmwood in Marshalltown, and Hyperion, Wakonda, and Glen Oaks courses in the Des Moines area. Dealers received tips from Lynn Blevins, University of Iowa golf coach, and played golf with Brad Lohaus, a former UI basketball player who played for the Milwaukee Bucs at the time. Jim Walden, ISU football coach, addressed the

IADA members annually headed to Washington, D.C., for NADA events and trips to see congressmen. On the hill in 1999 were John McEleney, Stan Moffitt, Eddie Elbert, and Marv Hartwig.

One of the highlights of the 1990 annual convention of the IADA was the idea exchange luncheon. Each participant was given three minutes to present his/her idea on making additional profits or cutting expenses in a dealership. After hearing all of the ideas, attendees voted for the best idea at their table. These winners then presented their ideas to the entire group, and an overall winner was determined. Here are the award-winning ideas from 1990.

$250 Grand-Prize Winner
Critiquing Lending Institutions
Rusty Jones, J.M. Jones & Sons, Inc., Manchester
"When we have a customer who needs to finance a new car, we submit the credit application to all of the lending institutions we currently work with. We keep track of the response from all six lending institutions, and at the end of each month we send out a 'report card.' The report card tells the lenders how many cars we have sold, how many of those cars were financed, and how many were financed by that particular lending institution. The report card has helped us get more cars financed through some of the lending institutions."

$50 Prize Winners
Customer of the Week
Mark Birdnow, Mark Birdnow Chevrolet, Jesup
"In a small town, this is an effective use of advertising money as well as a great way to get positive exposure. As well as being costly, special sale ads may happen to hit at a time when only one or two people are ready to buy. The 'customer of the week' ads keep telling people who you are, where you are, and that their neighbors, friends, and family are buying from you. Very simply, you ask either at delivery, or shortly thereafter if the buyers would like to be customer of the week. You run their picture with a few quotes on 'why I bought my car at Mark Birdnow's' in the newspaper. If possible, use well-known people such as the mayor. The picture is an effective attention grabber and gets customers talking about your dealership. The customer of the week program generates invaluable word-of-mouth advertising."

Minimizing Used Car Inventory
Jack Simonsen, Johnson Motor Company, Denison
"Every dealer recognizes the fact that the fresh used car trade-ins when properly reconditioned sell the quickest and at the greatest profits. To minimize the possibility of over-age used cars and trucks continuing to depreciate and accumulate additional lot expense, we adopted the following policy six years ago. We add $100 to the

inventory value of every used car or used truck trade-in. We do this after the new deal has been booked. This eliminates paying unearned commission on the $100. We then deduct $100 from the next oldest unit. By doing this, we make the unit more saleable. The used car managers and salespeople try to sell the units since there will be commissions to be made on profit and the managers will not have to sustain a loss in their department."

Improve Vehicle Sales Traffic Control
Roland Griffith, Griffith Ford-Lincoln-Mercury, Carroll
"We found that our salespeoples' traffic reports and management numbers were sometimes inconsistent. We were not able to effectively follow-up our UPs (customers) or calculate an accurate closing ratio. We decided to hire an additional sales employee to act as our hawk/greeter. Aside from several administrative duties, the main responsibility of the hawk/greeter is to monitor traffic on the premises and to control the flow of sales calls. The daily UP log is placed in the sales tower, where the hawk/greeter enforces the logging of all walk-in and phone UP of the salespeople and inputs the information into our computer UP database. Initially, we paid our hawk/greeter on a regular hourly rate. However, this was not incentive enough to monitor the traffic as closely as we wanted it monitored. With the new plan, the hawk/greeter is paid a lower hourly rate plus $1 per phone or walk-in UP that has been logged. The hawk works harder and the counts are more accurate. This plan has helped sales management attain more reliable records of the traffic through the dealership and also enabled us to calculate a more accurate closing ratio for each salesperson as well as the entire sales department."

Building Sales Team Spirit
Doug Schoon, Schoon's Auto and Truck Center, Anamosa
"We developed this program to create a much greater team effort in our sales department. Each salesperson is given their equal share of the dealership's monthly sales goal as an individual target. The salesperson is then given a $25 bonus per unit sold if they meet their monthly sales target and if the dealership meets its total monthly sales goal. This has resulted in the sales force working together and

trying harder to get their extra deal. The salespeople that are on top in sales for the month suddenly become a little more interested in helping the lower producers meet their goals. Each sale brings the store closer to its monthly sales goal and each person closer to their monthly bonus."

Self-Evaluations for Salespeople
Jim Hayden, Jim Hayden Ford-Mercury, Inc., Osage
"The self evaluation is a good training tool for beginners and an excellent reinforcer for the 'old sales pro.' We have our sales people fill out a self-evaluation form after they visit with a customer. They record what went right, what went wrong, why they settled on a certain vehicle, etc. They also analyze why they didn't get the sale and what type of follow-up plan they should have. We go over these evaluations at sales meetings. Other salespeople have a chance to offer suggestions and give advice. We find these evaluation sessions helpful for new or struggling salespeople, plus it reinforces the sales system we use and acts as a reminder to our salespeople to cover each step."

If You're Not Participating in Hawkeye Life,
It May Be Costing You Money
Jim Baier, Jim Baier, Inc., Fort Madison
"Hawkeye Life Insurance is designed to give maximum profit return to its participating dealers. Started in 1976, Hawkeye now has over 170 dealers doing more than $6.5 million of new premium in 1989. The company's current assets are over $11 million and growing. Hawkeye is managed by an executive staff and is closely governed by the board of directors, made up of 12 Iowa auto dealers. The Hawkeye staff is available to provide schools and seminars on a quarterly basis; assistance in selecting, recommending, and hiring F&I people; and assistance with complete monthly reporting. We have found Hawkeye Life Insurance to be an important tool for building profits and we encourage other dealers to take a look at what Hawkeye can do for your dealership."
–August 1990, *IADA Flash Facts Mini*

1995 IADA MEMBERSHIP SURVEY

- 71 percent of those responding drew customers from a population base of less than 30,000 and 29 percent serve a trade area of 30,000 or more. The median number of years of dealer ownership was approximately 23.
- Dealers' greatest concerns about their future profitability are focused primarily on manufacturer relations and the negative outcome of cost shifting and franchise interference. Some 90 percent said manufacturer relations was a bigger concern for the future viability of their dealership than state or federal regulations.
- The top three concerns for all dealers were increased operating

costs, low profit margins, and relationship with the manufacturer.
- Only 27 percent strongly agreed that in five years their dealership would be more profitable and stronger than it is today.
- Workers' compensation insurance and group health insurance were the highest rated services of IADA. They were graded "A" or "B" by more than 90 percent of the membership responding to the survey.
- 86 percent of those responding had consulted directly on matters with the IADA legal counsel and executive director.
–Letter from Gary Thomas, IADA Executive Vice President, January 25, 1996

golfers after their day on the course in 1991. That year, a fall outing was also held to raise funds for DEAC/ICAR. Ron Nanke, IADA's director of field operations, took home a set of Mizuno irons for his hole-in-one on the 7th hole at Hyperion in 1992.

In 1995, the golf event became a fundraiser for the new IAD Foundation with $100 of each registration going directly to the foundation. Some $10,000 was raised with the first golfing event. In each of the years that followed, IADA's golf outing raised money for scholarships for those choosing to train for a career in the automotive business.

Legislative

In July of 1990, IADA's top two legislative concerns for the year became law. First, manufacturers could not require dealers to submit to mandatory binding arbitration. Second, the dealer bond was increased to

$35,000. IADA's efforts to pass a title branding law failed that year. Such legislation would enable consumers—and dealers—to know that a vehicle had formerly been on a salvage certificate of title. Since the value of a vehicle with a branded title was thousands of dollars less than one without a brand, a "rebuilt" notation was important.

Title branding remained a priority in 1991 but did not pass. However, that year Iowa's Dealer Bill of Rights was "quietly" amended so that a manufacturer could not reduce a dealer's area of responsibility without a hearing. To help move the association's concerns forward in 1992, IADA held 23 legislative meetings in November, 1991. Some 200 dealers gathered with 90 legislators to share the Iowa industry's most critical issues. Title branding and damage disclosure legislation passed in 1992, the same year that IADA fought DOT's proposal to take over titling and registrations from county treasurers.

Legislative issues with leased vehicles were prominent by 1995, and IADA was successful with laws that addressed lease advertising, damage disclosure on leased vehicles, owner's liability on leased vehicles, and whether the copy of the lease was to be kept with the vehicle.

Leasing was a popular method of financing vehicles during the mid-'90s. However, Iowa taxed leased vehicles the same as purchased vehicles, even though the lease customer might have use of the vehicles for as little as a year. The lease tax bill passed in 1996 and was amended in 1997 to make it clear that there was no "tax on the tax."

Rusty Jones, Dean Beecher, Dan Kruse, Vinje Dahl, and Don Pierson were among those present for the 1997 summer board meeting.

Iowa New Car AND TRUCK DEALERS

A chart included with a membership mailing provided the number of dealers in Iowa at 10-year intervals, beginning in 1969 and ending in 1999. While dealer numbers were listed by county, the total numbers for Iowa tell the story:1969–1,978 dealers, 1979–888 dealers, 1989–520 dealers, 1999–443 dealers.

Three counties—Decatur, Freemont and Van Buren—no longer had dealerships by 1989, having dropped from six, four and two dealers in 1969. The six counties that had gained one to three dealers between 1989 and 1999 were Cerro Gordo (8 to 9),

Cherokee (4 to 5), Ida (4 to 5), Keokuk (2 to 3), Polk (28 to 31) and Woodbury (11 to 13). All had suffered losses in at least one previous decade so that each of those counties gaining between 1989 and1999 suffered a net loss over the 40-year period.

The lowest number of dealers lost across the four decades was Polk County with one; the greatest was 13 dealers in Kossuth County. Thirteen counties recorded double-digit losses in number of dealers. The average number lost was 6.4 dealerships.
–May 28, 1999, *Action Update*

In 1996, IADA worked closely with Iowa's DOT for new rules regarding business hours, display facilities, and license applications, which went into effect in August. In 1998, IADA was successful with revisions to the damage disclosure law and in eliminating confusion on auto insurance card requirements. That year companies received some immunity from penalties for offenses discovered in environmental self-audits through Iowa's Environmental Audit Privilege and Immunity Act. Legislative changes to Iowa's three-day cooling off rule were needed by 1999, since this situation had been complicated by Internet sales. Warranty legislation that passed that year set a 12-month limit on chargebacks as a result of factory warranty audits, and the vehicle registration bill signed into law gave dealers more time to submit papers to their country treasurers.

People

Eddie Elbert took another term as Iowa's NADA director beginning in 1991 and was elected to a two-year term as regional vice president and thus to the NADA Executive Committee. He chaired the 1995 NADA convention in Dallas, served on the NADA Guide Book committee and was a trustee on the NAD Charitable Foundation. Elbert was re-elected to represent the state for a third term beginning in 1994.

John O. Falb was honored in 1992 for his chairmanship of DEAC and ICAR and for raising more than $100,000 since 1990 for political action activities. When Elbert declined to run again after 12 years as Iowa's NADA director, Falb was elected to his first three-year term in 1997. The NADA director position became an ex-officio board position in April, 1996.

In November, 1998, the board approved the addition of a seat for a member who represented the heavy truck industry. At the next election in April, 1999, Bill McKenna joined the governing body.

In 1999, Charlie Zook, Charlie Zook Motors, Inc. and Charlie Zook Mitsubishi, Sioux City, became the second Iowa auto dealer to win the prestigious national TIME Magazine Quality Dealer of the Year Award. Zook, who had dedicated 40 years of his life to the auto industry, was president of IADA in 1978, and in 1988 was vice president and founding board member of the IAD Foundation.

If You're Not Participating in Hawkeye Life, It May Be Costing You Money

Jim Baier, Jim Baier, Inc., Fort Madison

"Hawkeye Life Insurance is designed to give maximum profit return to its participating dealers. Started in 1976, Hawkeye now has more than 170 dealers doing more than $6.5 million of new premium in 1989. The company's current assets are over $11 million and growing. Hawkeye is managed by an executive staff and is closely governed by the board of directors, made up of 12 Iowa auto dealers. The Hawkeye staff is available to provide schools and seminars on a quarterly basis; assistance in selecting, recommending, and hiring F&I people; and assistance with complete monthly reporting. We have found Hawkeye Life Insurance to be an important tool for building profits and we encourage other dealers to take a look at what Hawkeye can do for your dealership."

—August 1990, *IADA Flash Facts Mini*

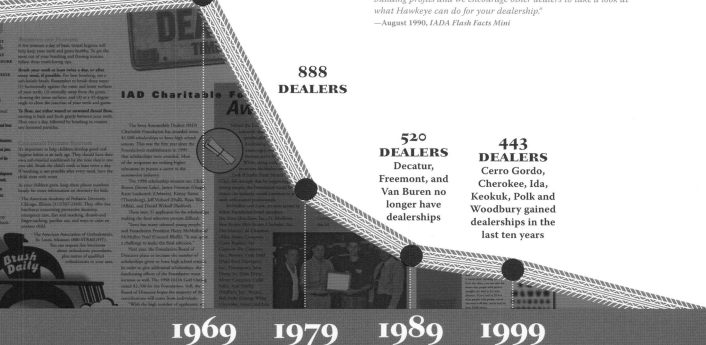

1,978 DEALERS

888 DEALERS

520 DEALERS
Decatur, Freemont, and Van Buren no longer have dealerships

443 DEALERS
Cerro Gordo, Cherokee, Ida, Keokuk, Polk and Woodbury gained dealerships in the last ten years

1969   1979   1989   1999

Named honorary IADA members in the 1990s were H.E. Morrison, Jr., Stuart (1990), Warren McEleney, Clinton (1994), and Lee Holt, Spencer (1998). At the 1994 convention, McEleney, who had served as NADA president but never held that post within IADA, was named IADA's first and only honorary president to date.

Public Image

Efforts by dealers to do good things for their communities and the people of Iowa continued throughout the state.

In cooperation with the NAD Charitable Foundation, IADA continued to present cardiopulmonary resuscitation (CPR) mannequins—adult and junior sizes—to entities throughout Iowa. By the end of the decade they had placed 80 units in hospitals, and with Red Cross units and service organizations throughout Iowa. Seven of the mannequins were resuscitation babies, donated to celebrate the Des Moines birth of the first set of surviving septuplets—the McCaugheys. Proud pop Kenny McCaughey was an employee of Wright Chevrolet, Carlisle, at the time of their November, 1997, delivery.

In 1991, Iowa dealers and their employees raised $500 for Operation Home Front, an American Red Cross program to assist Iowa families of soldiers serving in the Persian Gulf. Dealer interest in the program and individual donations continued. Noble Ford Mercury of Indianola donated $9,000 for Persian Gulf families, $100 for each retail unit sold in February.

The 1995 IADA Executive Committee included Gary Thomas, secretary; Don Pierson, president; Stew Hansen, past president; Vinje Dahl, first vice president; and Dan Kruse, second vice president.

Also in 1991, IDOT identified five communities that had low useage of child safety seats. Five dealers in those areas held child passenger safety clinics at their dealerships for daycare providers, preschool teachers, and public health and law enforcement officials. They were R.K. Belt and Sons of Red Oak; Wagler Motor Co. of Sigourney; Bevins Motor Co., Inc., of Belle Plaine; Kemna Oldsmobile of Algona; and Elbert Motor Co. of Pocahontas. In 1999, dealers sponsored child safety seat inspections in collaboration with the Iowa Department of Health. Some 450 seats were inspected, and 95 percent misuse was found.

IADA members joined forces to raise more than $10,000 for the Iowa Special Olympics in 1995. Donating dealers sponsored special-needs athletes from their counties. Employees at Stew Hansen's Dodge City raised more than $2,000 for the program. To celebrate Iowa's Sesquicentennial in 1996, IADA became one of eight corporate sponsors of Motor Ioway, a 1,000-mile motor tour for classic vehicles held in October. IADA has continued its sponsorship each year of the vintage vehicle tours and related events.

Services

IADA Services began offering a Motor Vehicle Records Check Service early in the decade and expanded its forms department and phone service in 1993. A prescription drug card program and an employee assistance program (EAP) for dealerships were added in 1994. IADA Services began offering "not for sale" static stickers, damage disclosure statement forms for leased cars, and goodwill service forms. In 1997, the retail installment contract form and three-day notice of cancellation forms were revised to comply with changes in the law.

In 1995, IADA's group health insurance program had 335 dealerships enrolled and 443 companies were in the workers' compensation program. These two programs were the highest rated services by the membership in the 1995 IADA survey. After several years of lower workers' compensation rates—reaching a 30 percent discount by 1998—and returns on premium averaging 20 percent per year, no dividends were paid in 1999.

IADA put its first Web site on the Internet in 1994 and began the first major improvement to the site—online access to the Ratebook—in August, 1997. The association also began assisting dealerships in the purchase of corporate apparel and in 1999 introduced an online catalog.

In 1998, IADA began including a monthly "Health TuneUp" newsletter with the IADA Action Update and published a colorful quarterly newsletter, *Dealer Times*. In 1999, to help dealers prepare for Y2K, IADA provided a three-part report addressing the potential computer problems that could affect dealerships in the change to a new millennium.

After three years of soliciting members for money for IADA's legal defense fund, dealer contributions were put to use in 1998. Arenson Chevrolet, Center Point, was sold to RAM Automotive, a corporation partly owned by long-time Arenson general manager Rick Rojek. Chevrolet refused to honor the transfer, and RAM filed for an injunction in federal court. IADA attorneys intervened, and a settlement was reached just minutes before the hearing was to begin. IADA reimbursed RAM for a large portion of its legal expenses pursuant to guidelines adopted by the board.

In 1999, the legal defense fund helped Riley Auto Sales, Dubuque, win a franchise battle with Mazda after moving its dealership to a better location. Mazda attempted to terminate the franchise agreement in a hearing before the Iowa Department of Inspections and Appeals. Riley won because of a recent amendment to the Iowa Dealer Franchise Law. IADA called it "a great victory that could benefit all Iowa dealers," encouraged dealers to contribute again to the fund, and asked them "to let the factories know that Iowa dealers will not be pushed around."

Manufacturer Relations

At the middle of the decade, the IADA membership survey—completed by 242 dealers—found the dealers' greatest concerns about their future profitability were manufacturer relations, cost shifting, and franchise

Attending a 1998 IADA board meeting were John Falb, Eddie Elbert, Marv Hartwig, and Warren McEleney.

interference. Almost 90 percent believed that manufacturer relations was a bigger problem for the viability of their dealerships than state or federal regulations.

Before the end of the decade, GM announced its intention to purchase 10 percent of GM dealerships over ten years in the top 130 markets. In November, 1999, the IADA board set its main legislative priority for 2000: to prohibit manufacturers from owning dealerships in Iowa. The board directed staff to set up a series of meetings between dealers and legislators to discuss the association's 2000 legislative program. In December, IADA held 16 town meetings throughout the state to give dealers an opportunity to share their thoughts about the unfair competition that manufacturers create when owning dealerships and the need for legislation to prevent such competition.

Annual Contributions OF IOWA'S NEW-VEHICLE DEALERS

Iowa's dealers maintain a multi-billion dollar retail industry.
• Average sales per dealership: $12.118 million
• Total sales of all new-vehicle dealerships in Iowa: $5.392 billion
• Dealership sales as % of total retail sales in the state: 21.7%
• Estimated number of new-vehicle dealerships: 445

Dealers provide thousands of well-paying jobs in Iowa.
• Total number of new-vehicle dealership employees in Iowa: 12,729
• Average number of employees per dealership: 29

• Average annual earnings of new-vehicle dealership employees: $31,356
• Dealership payroll as % of total state retail payroll: 11.4%
• Annual payroll of new-vehicle dealerships: $390 million
• Average annual payroll per new-vehicle dealership: $880,000
–NADA figures for economic activity in 1998, reported September 24, 1999, *Action Update*

TO GLENDA MILLARD

In 1986, when Glenda Millard had been a Ford truck dealer for one month, she attended her first Ford truck sales meeting in Orlando. Her presence among the dealers—aboard a bus bound for the Ford test track—was so unexpected that she was told three times to leave the dealer bus and please board the spouse bus to Sea World. When the tour director finally approached her seat, Glenda simply said, "Not all dealers are men anymore."

For her first two awards for outstanding accounting from Ford, Glenda received a tie tack and cigar humidor. Her placecard at a Ford banquet table once read: "Mr. Glenda Millard and Guest." She was always in the minority during her career, but Glenda was no stranger to meeting challenges.

It was a skill she developed since the beginning. Born with spina bifida, Glenda endured surgery at Mayo Clinic—which she credits with saving her life—and was told she'd spend that life in a wheelchair. She learned to walk when her mother simply told her to get up and make walking her physical therapy. Through her high school years Glenda wore leg braces, and she credits her parents with teaching her to stand up and face obstacles. When she left her hometown of Waverly to attend the American Institute of Business (AIB) in Des Moines in 1957, her gift from her father was a $2 bill. "I was on my own, and he told me if I never spent that two dollar bill I'd never be broke," said Glenda. "I still have it." Glenda has added a few more dollars to that nest egg through her successful career. She was the first woman office manager of a dealership in Des Moines in the 1960s and the first woman stockholder of a Ford truck dealership in the U.S. in 1986.

In 1958, after AIB, Glenda took a job as a secretary with Hawkeye Truck Equipment Company at 9th and Keo in Des Moines and started learning accounting. The company sold truck equipment, school buses, and funeral coaches. In 1962 when Ford wanted the dealership to become one of a dozen truck centers in the nation, the business moved to East 14th Street and became Hawkeye Ford. The firm went through numerous owners and managers before a general manager—a CPA—made Glenda his office manager. Her accounting knowledge grew, and so did many other skills. In 1970 she moved to Charles Gabus Ford and in 1975 to Mid-States Truck Sales, Inc., where she became secretary-treasurer of the truck dealership. In 1986 the dealership was owned by Dick McFall, who was ready to sell. When he told Glenda about the out-of-state individual who was interested in buying, Glenda she said she could never work for that man because of his ethics. "Then buy it yourself," was McFall's response.

That night Glenda told her husband, Dick, of her conversation with McFall. Dick said, "You've been running it in the background. Go for it." She called long-time acquaintance Marv Perry that evening to see if he was interested in buying Mid-States Truck Center with her. "He laughed and said he was going to call me the next day to see if I had any interest in a partnership with him," said Glenda.

The Millard's life savings went into Glenda's percentage of the ownership she shared with Perry. "In 20 years," she said, "Marv and I never had a major argument. We were like brother and sister, and were always on the same wavelength. Neither one of us had a college degree but just learned the industry through hard work."

With another partner in 1997, Glenda and Marv purchased Oliver Motor in Osceola, and in 1999 Glenda and Marv purchased Mitchell Motor Company, a Ford dealership, in Adel. (It became Mid-States Ford, Inc., in 2003.) In 2001, they sold the Osceola dealership to their partner, sold off their truck operation, combined their Adel dealership with a truck franchise, and began building in Waukee. Glenda and Marv sold their dealership in June, 2006.

While Glenda was always in the minority, she was no stranger to 60- to 80-hour work weeks and said, "I always had the respect of the men." Her groundbreaking efforts and ability to conquer challenges were featured in *The Des Moines Register* in 1994. "A local school teacher sent me a laminated copy of that article when she retired," said Glenda. "She said that for eleven years she'd used my story as an example of persistence in life."

Of Marv Perry, pictured here with Glenda, Glenda says, "In 20 years, Marv and I never had a major argument."

Glenda was surrounded by her peers on the front of *The Des Moines Register* Classified Section in 1986. Pictured are
A. Chuck Betts
B. Clair Conway
C. Bud Mulcahy
D. Wes Jordan
E. Dave Wright
F. Carl Wilson
G. Don Beneventi
H. Brent Hansen
I. Steve Pershing
J. Gene Gabus
K. Ken Gookin
L. Lowell Schlesimen
M. Marv Perry
N. Glenda Millard
O. Charles Gabus
P. Mike Wagler
Q. Allen Wagler
R. Mark Vukovich
S. Max Holmes
T. Mark Schneider
U. Jim Senftner
V. Steve Wood
W. Royce Buckwalter
X. Jim Clark
Y. Jerry Watters
Z. John Ramsey

"I was on my own, and he told me if I never spent that two dollar bill I'd never be broke," said Glenda. "I still have it."

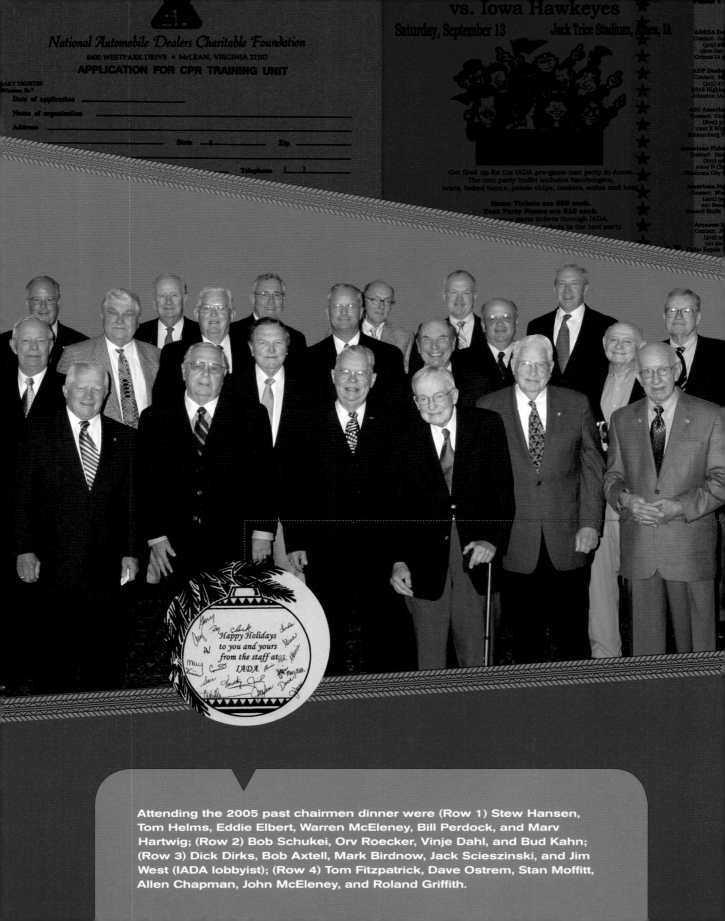

Attending the 2005 past chairmen dinner were (Row 1) Stew Hansen, Tom Helms, Eddie Elbert, Warren McEleney, Bill Perdock, and Marv Hartwig; (Row 2) Bob Schukei, Orv Roecker, Vinje Dahl, and Bud Kahn; (Row 3) Dick Dirks, Bob Axtell, Mark Birdnow, Jack Scieszinski, and Jim West (IADA lobbyist); (Row 4) Tom Fitzpatrick, Dave Ostrem, Stan Moffitt, Allen Chapman, John McEleney, and Roland Griffith.

Des Moines' finest golf courses.

Register today for the 2002 IADA Golf Outing

Monday, June 17, 2002
Des Moines Golf & Country Club, West Des Moines

the 2000s

"The mission of the Iowa Auto Dealers Association
is to protect, preserve, and increase the value of the
motor vehicle franchise system and to provide needed
support and services to all member dealerships."

–Mission Statement, Adopted in 2002

Survey of FORD-LINCOLN-MERCURY DEALERS

Within the last month, IADA took a survey of Iowa Ford, Lincoln and Mercury dealers. We wanted to see what the support was for the association's continued involvement in the 17-state coalition fighting the two-tier pricing aspect of Blue Oval, Lincoln Premiere and Mercury Advantage. Out of 140 dealers, 95 told IADA to keep up the fight, 11 told IADA to back off, and the rest did not vote. Other states are seeing similar results. Meanwhile, Ford continues to urge its dealers to ask state associations to back off. Ford reports that 80 percent of dealers are certified and should get paid later this month. IADA will do another survey to identify the Iowa dealers who are not certified and will not get paid.

– April 19, 2001, *Action Update*

(NOTE: Ford discontinued payout to Blue Oval dealers in March, 2005.)

The trust that existed between dealers and manufacturers had all but disappeared as the 1990s ended, due to announcements by Ford and General Motors that they intended to expand their presence as retailers. Dealers were skeptical when, in early 2000, both companies changed their plans. General Motors reversed its proposal to buy up to 700 dealerships in the top 130 markets, and Ford said it now intended to use dealers as its only source of distribution.

IADA's top legislative priority for 2000 remained unchanged: to prevent motor vehicle manufacturers from obtaining a dealer's license in Iowa. IADA stated, "This is a dealer license issue, not a franchise issue," and provided its members with talking points for grassroots communication with legislators. Iowa was the first state to get its manufacturer-ownership bill enacted, with a July 1, 2000, implementation date.

Other issues strained relationships between factories and dealers. IADA and the majority of its Ford-Lincoln-Mercury dealers rallied against the two-tiered pricing aspects of programs such as Ford's Blue Oval, Lincoln's Premier, and Mercury's Advantage. Ford viewed its system as "a fair and reasonable customer satisfaction incentive program in which all dealers could participate." IADA and 24 other associations that became part of the Blue Oval Coalition felt dealers were asked to jump through hoops to get an extra 1.25 percent off invoice. This "troublesome requirement" threatened a "pro-consumer, franchise automotive retail system that allocated and priced vehicles in a fair, equitable and non-discriminatory manner."

IADA 2007 chairman Phil Weber (center) and Gary Thomas, president, spent many days during summer and fall of 2007 on Iowa roads calling upon IADA members. Their stops included a visit to Lauterbach Buick-Pontiac in Newton to visit with Jason (left) and Dean Lauterbach (right). Discussions with dealers primarily focused on the general condition of the industry, federal issues impacting dealers, and compliance with state rules and regulations.

IADA raised funds to fight Blue Oval. The same proportion of non-Ford dealers contributed as Ford dealers, suggesting that all dealers recognized the threat of price discrimination to their businesses. Pooled with other associations, the funds were used to pursue legal action against Ford-Lincoln-Mercury for violation of federal anti-trust laws. In 2005, Ford withdrew the program after North Carolina dealers won the first round of their own lawsuit. Most of the money raised was returned to the contributing Iowa dealers, but 20 dealers either left their money in the legal defense fund or transferred it to the IAD Foundation.

Legal defense funds were used to fight manufacturers' "right of first refusal" in a case involving Bob Zimmerman Ford, Cedar Rapids. The dealership had a buy-sell agreement in 2000 for its BMW franchise, but BMW fought the sale. The Iowa Supreme Court confirmed in 2004 that while there is "right of first refusal" in the BMW franchise, it did not apply in Iowa due to provisions of the Iowa Franchise Law.

In 2005, the association struggled to maintain a position of neutrality on the issue of a dealer's right to move without factory approval. The issue was complicated by the fact that the association had members who supported the legislation and others who opposed it. In other issues, IADA worked with GM and Chrysler dealers when factories assigned new areas of responsibility that reduced dealer territories. The right to a hearing before an administrative law judge was set out in Iowa's Dealer Franchise Law, which also blocked GM's strategy to sue dealers who refused to move non-GM brands out of their GM showrooms. IADA also helped stop an unfair Chrysler Jeep program in 2005 but was unsuccessful in fighting Jaguar's termination of a Des Moines dealership in 2000.

Other Legislation
In 2001, the passage of HF 325 allowed IADA's health plan to remain exempt from the two percent insurance premium tax. The association's main piece of legislation, HF 324, protected a dealer's right to sell the franchise, a law needed in light of the Jaguar decision in 2000. A flat vehicle registration rate for older vehicles also passed, as did changes needed in Iowa's lemon law.

In 2002, a decline in state revenues had IADA successfully fighting those who wanted to divert road use tax revenues from the sale of new and used cars and trucks into the general fund for other expenditures. IADA also further clarified "right of first refusal" in the Iowa

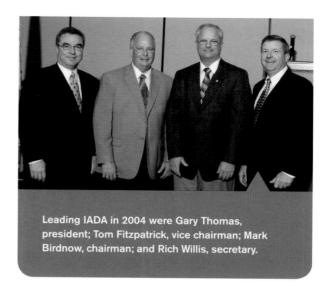
Leading IADA in 2004 were Gary Thomas, president; Tom Fitzpatrick, vice chairman; Mark Birdnow, chairman; and Rich Willis, secretary.

Code, secured legislation that required trade-in customers to disclose their knowledge of prior or current damage to a vehicle, and fixed a damage disclosure loophole.

In 2003, GAP insurance coverage was expressly legalized, and the damage disclosure limit requirement rose to $6,000. In 2004, IADA supported a change in the disclosure limit to 50 percent or more of a vehicle's value at the time of a wreck. A tougher service contract law was enacted in 2004.

After elections in 2006, with 22 new legislators set to enter the statehouse in 2007, IADA began identifying its new legislative connections. The success of its legislative program over the years was due in part to personal relationships with individual lawmakers by local automobile dealers. The association's grassroots efforts for members to connect with new legislators was as solid as ever, and as in the past, all legislators were invited to the annual fall town meetings in Council Bluffs, Des Moines, Cedar Rapids, and Davenport.

The 2007 session marked the first time in 30 years that Democrats controlled both houses and the governor's office, and many new issues came to the forefront. These included "right to work," choice of physician in workers' compensation claims, and tax issues that affected vehicle pricing.

Insurance
On November 1, 2000, IADA changed health care providers from Federated to Wellmark Blue Cross/Blue Shield for "the best PPO network in the state." While there was a 13.5 percent increase on the medical plan rates, those for life, dental and disability insurance did

M.O. "Bud" Kahn, Bob Axtell, and LeNore and
Stew Hansen enjoyed memories shared at IADA's
2005 past presidents' dinner.

not change. Although some enrolled dealers dropped the IADA plan—primarily to stay with Federated—40 percent were back by August, 2001. In 2002, more than 1,400 new members joined the plan. Benefits were enhanced, an HMO alternative was added, and enrollment grew more than 52 percent to generate more than $2.3 million of premium per month by 2007. The insurance trust at that time offered 18 different plans to fit the needs of individual dealerships. It was being used by 250 member stores, covering 10,000 employees and their dependents.

IADA Services

Martha Martell, staff legal counsel for IADA, retired in 2006 after 21years with the association.

In 2001, the IADA workers' compensation program began rating dealerships individually, according to loss history, and in 2002 named "All-Star" dealers that had five years of outstanding safety history. In 2006, IADA teamed with Farm Bureau and Ken Strosahl to offer safety consultation to dealerships agreeing to two sessions with Strosahl. By the end of 2006, when much of the industry was seeing a rate hike of 10 percent, IADA's average workers' compensation increase was one-half of one percent.

By 2007, IADA's workers' compensation program had existed for 50 years—the last 20 with Farm Bureau as its reinsurer. Some 225 dealerships—more than half of Iowa's dealerships—were insured, generating $3.7 million in premiums in 2007.

Special rates with United Parcel Service—as much as 50 percent off other carriers—were created for dealers in early 2000 through IADA Services. The IADA-MCI/World Com long-distance program became IADA-VerizonBusiness. By November, 2006, the association was billing more than $600,000 a month for phone services and still saving money for dealers. In 2001, a new partnership with First National Bank, Omaha, Merchant Card Processing Division provided credit card processing. By late 2006, the program was being used by 35 percent of member dealerships.

The IADA board approved development of a database maintenance and marketing alliance in 2003. Through volume-pricing advantages, members could purchase office products, furniture, computer supplies, and promotional products through Boise Office Solutions at substantial savings.

In June, 2005, IADA began a partnership with the Iowa Waste Reduction Center (IWRC), conducting a study of wastes commonly generated in the automotive repair industry and specifically in Iowa dealerships. All service departments were asked to participate in the collection of samples of waste such as antifreeze, floor dry, and sump sludge. Preliminary results—which could benefit dealers around the nation—were released in the summer of 2007. The IWRC in 2005 also began providing pertinent articles for *Action Update* on such topics as managing oil-absorbent waste, environmental advice for all Iowa businesses, fluorescent bulb management, paint hazards, and sump sludge.

In 2005, the association's *Action Update* outlined a five-step privacy safeguards program to comply with new federal regulations concerning the privacy of customers' financial information.

Early in the millennium, IADA installed direct phone lines to each staff member. It also launched a third-generation Web site in March, 2000, with information for dealership employees and the general public. New features provided dealers with the most timely and useful materials, products, and services. Site visitors could purchase shop supplies, automotive parts, body shop supplies, tires, and specialty items, as well as shop for forms and promotional products. Soon, downloadable documents, access to human resources information, guides on insurance purchasing, and advice on safety programs were included. In 2003, an online legal library—now with more than 180 articles—became part of the members-only, password-protected area of the site, which also included the IADA Ratebook for updated vehicle registration fees. The Iowa Department of Transportation began maintaining and posting this information in 2005.

By 2000, more than 60 percent of dealers had e-mail addresses, and nearly 50 percent had Web sites. Some 71 percent felt the *Action Update* should be sent by e-mail, a change carried out in May, 2001. [Past issues of *Action Update* are archived and searchable on the association Web site in the members-only section.] By mid-2004, paper copies of *Action Update* no longer were sent to dealerships.

IADA found itself moving away from providing certain forms in 2000 when the Iowa Department of Transportation began putting its forms online. In 2004, the association translated its two most popular forms—the car purchase order form and retail installment contract—into Spanish. The business forms area of IADA Services, which had sales of more than $2 million in 2001, continued to shrink in the electronic age. IADA's challenge continues to be protecting its copyrights while providing a service to its dealer members. In September, 2006, IADA terminated its 14-year relationship for automotive business forms

with Reynolds and Reynolds. Unburdened by an exclusive agreement, IADA's Printing and Promotions Department began shopping more suppliers and vendors to find the right products for individual dealerships. In January, 2007, the staff cited an example of saving a dealer $2,300 on 12 items that previously would have been purchased from its exclusive supplier.

IADA Services also began offering members a personalized employment manual that complied with current state and federal laws. It also reflected choices made by dealers about policies and procedures for their facilities. Each time laws change to impact dealer operations, IADA notifies dealerships.

Charitable Donations and Goodwill

Through the NAD Charitable Foundation, IADA continued to present Rescusci Anne CPR mannequins. From 2000 to 2007, these went to ambulance services in Carroll and Britt; four Red Cross chapters (Gateway, North Central, Des Moines County, and Ames); the YMCA in Council Bluffs, Dubuque Mercy Medical

Each year IADA and NADA jointly present 12 Rescusci Anne CPR training units to Iowa communities. Collectively, these units help train and save more than 17,000 lives. Red Cross representatives from throughout the state who attended the 2006 spring board meeting to receive the units from their communities were Kristi O'Brien (Waterloo), Nicole Vermeer (Marshalltown), Jennifer Ranhiem (Mason City), Stephanie Kappos (Mason City), Mark Smoot (Ottumwa), Carol White (Fort Madison), Ruth Randleman (Carlisle), Mary Post (Fort Dodge), MaryAnn Sinkler (Des Moines), Rhonda McGarry (Sioux City), and Ginnie Weber (Cedar Rapids). Dealers present were Jeff Finch (Grinnell), Mike Clemons (Marshalltown), Doug and Deb Vermeer (Montezuma), Bill Colwell, Jr. (Hudson), Rich Willis (Des Moines), Mark Birdnow (Jesup), Brad Deery (Maquoketa), and Chad VanNess (Ottumwa). Not Pictured: Becky Steinbacher of Mahaska County Red Cross.

Center, and Dubuque Middle School. Twelve additional mannequins were presented in Waterloo, Marshalltown, Mason City, Ottumwa, Fort Madison, Carlisle, Fort Dodge, Des Moines, Cedar Rapids, and Mahaska County.

In 2001, the NAD Charitable Foundation began offering automated external defibrillator units to dealers who wanted to donate them to rescue units in their communities. When Iowa's county treasurers solicited donations for a raffle to support a scholarship fund for children of county employees, more than $10,000 of the $40,000 raised came from 99 Iowa dealers. The raffle winner won $15,000 and chose to purchase a vehicle from Harlan Auto Mart.

Golf
Annual IADA golfing events continue to focus on raising money for Foundation scholarships. Since 2000, dealers and their friends have golfed at sell-out outings at Hyperion, Des Moines Golf and Country Club, Glen Oaks (Des Moines and West Des Moines), The Harvester (Rhodes), and the Tournament Club of Iowa (Polk City). By 2006, they'd raised approximately $30,000 in the new millennium.

Washington, D.C., Trips for Dealers
For many years, Iowa dealers and IADA staff have attended NADA's fall lobbying events in Washington. The point of the meetings is to learn about NADA's legislative priorities and to visit Iowa's congressional delegation. But the 2001 dealer meeting was the gathering Iowans would

Calling on former Iowa Congressman Jim Nussle (third from left) during an NADA fall dealer gathering were John Falb, Jack Scieszinski, Nussle, Rusty Jones, and Marianne and George Grask. Nussle later became director of the White House Office of Management and Budget.

never forget; it was cancelled during an opening breakfast. "I was chair of IADA then, and we had 17 people—including spouses—in Washington, D.C., on September 11 when terrorists attacked," said John McEleney, Clinton. "The weekend before, four couples had been in New York, and the last thing we looked at from the train we took to Washington was the twin towers.

"Senator J.C. Watts of Oklahoma was the NADA breakfast speaker, and we were less than one mile from the White House," McEleney said. "The speaker was interrupted, the members of Congress were taken away to bunkers, and we went to our rooms to turn on the televisions. Al Chapman, Gary Thomas, and I went out to look for ATM machines, and the streets were jammed with people. There were lines of people trying to rent cars. I'll never forget it."

A Washington, D.C., dealership came to the rescue of the stranded Iowa delegation, which purchased four vans outside the beltway, left at 5:30 a.m. on September 12, and caravanned home to Iowa together.

In 2002, the NADA fall D.C. meeting was attended by seven dealers and three staff members. After visits from IADA representatives, Iowa's entire congressional delegation signed on to co-sponsor a bill eliminating the mandatory binding arbitration provisions in manufacturers' contracts.

In 2005, NADA marked the thirtieth anniversary of its fall dealer meetings. That year seven Iowa dealers and staff attended. The 31st trip—in 2006—was attended by auto dealers from every congressional district in Iowa.

Other Meetings
IADA sponsored vehicle registration and unclaimed property meetings for finance and insurance managers when the state treasurer began to require annual unclaimed property reports. Some 40 percent of IADA members and 85 percent of county treasurers now attend the seminars.

In 2002, IADA offered a six-month "next generation" dealers training program. It was designed for younger dealers and managers preparing for a leadership position within a dealership, new dealer principals, and persons wanting networking opportunities with others at the same career stage. Participants met once a month, ending with a two-day event at the 2003 annual meeting. Those who completed the program were Jeremy Birdnow, Birdnow Motor Trade, Oelwein; Jeff Finch, Wes Finch Auto Plaza, Inc., Grinnell; Stacie Gustafson, Lake Chevrolet, Inc., Clear Lake; Eric Hoak, Hoak Motors, Inc., Sioux City; Jim Jensen, Crescent Chevrolet, Inc., Des Moines; Donna

Keim, Buysse Dodge, Inc., Davenport; Jason Lauterbach, Lauterbach Buick-Pontiac, Newton; Curtis Mack, John Falb Co., West Union; Angela Navrkal, Larson Motor Center, Inc., Onawa; Jason Schuelke, Schuelke Auto Co., Storm Lake; Chuck Walsh, Lou Walsh Motors, Inc., Carroll; Aaron Walter, Gib Walter Motors, Inc., Glenwood; Paul White, George White Chevrolet-Pontiac, Ames; Danny Wilson, Wilson Olds Cadillac Toyota, Ames; and Kevin Wittrock, Wittrock Motor Co., Carroll. Next Generation training is now offered in a two-and-a-half-day hands-on workshop by NADA and IADA.

In addition to workplace safety meetings and a session on how to survive a dealer audit, IADA and partners brought dealers comprehensive finance and insurance training, a menu selling school, a successorship seminar, truth-in-lending seminars, and human resources guideline seminars to help dealerships cope with laws on employment, discrimination, and workers' compensation.

In 2006 IADA began offering management retreats for dealers, general managers, sales managers, and service managers. Each of these intensive training and leadership sessions combined to provide dealers with strategies for having their most successful year ever.

DEAC/ICAR

As the decade began, IADA successfully surpassed a goal of $50,000 for ICAR and $20,350 for DEAC. In 2001, an August phone bank campaign to contact dealers who hadn't sent pledges resulted in raising more than $39,000 for DEAC and more than $25,000 for ICAR. ICAR consistently ranks among the 15 most influential PACs in the state. In 2006, under the longtime chairmanship of Eddie Elbert, DEAC/ICAR raised more than $74,000 and had 215 dealers contributing. With the death of Eddie Elbert in early 2007, Stan Moffitt took over leadership of this effort, and the association dedicated the campaign to its longtime chair.

People

John McEleney, McEleney Auto Center, Clinton, was named Iowa's NADA Director in February, 2003, becoming the second generation of McEleneys to represent Iowa at the national level. He replaced John Falb, John Falb Co., West Union, who had represented the state for six years. McEleney served on NADA's industry relations, government relations, and public affairs committees, and he regularly shared reports with the membership and sought their input in IADA's *Action Update*. He began a second term as the state's NADA director in February, 2006, and in 2007 expressed his intention to seek the national chairmanship. He was chosen to move forward to NADA's top leadership position.

The IADA board voted in 2004 to add an associate member seat that would be filled by an independent used-car dealer. Gary Septer was elected to that new voting position in 2005.

In April, 2006, George Grask, owner of Cedar Rapids Truck Center, began a two-year term as chairman of the American Truck Dealers, a 2,400-member group that is a division of NADA. This leader of the only national organization representing dealers selling new medium- and heavy-duty trucks also served as heavy-duty truck director on the IADA board.

Several outstanding individuals became honorary members of IADA between 2004 and 2007: Bob Axtell, formerly Axtell Motors, Newton; Al Chapman, Allen Motor Company, Cedar Falls; Eddie Elbert, Elbert Motor Company, Algona, and Elbert Chevrolet, Inc., Whittemore; John Falb, John Falb Company, West Union; Harry McMullen, McMullen Ford, Inc., Council Bluffs; and Jim West, Nyemaster Law Firm, Des Moines.

Two dealerships have been recognized for a century or more of service in Iowa. They are Allen Motor Company, Cedar Rapids (originally Elkader), and Kemmann

Father-and-Son LEADERSHIP TEAMS

When Phil Weber of Dubuque became IADA's chairman of the board at the association's 2007 annual meeting, he was following in the footsteps of his father, Les, who led IADA in 1971. The Webers are the second father and son team to hold IADA presidencies. In 1935, Floyd E. Hughes, Sr., Council Bluffs, was the top officer, and his son, Floyd Hughes Jr., served as association president in 1966.

Some of the major contributors to the IAD Foundation for Education in 2004 attended the winter board meeting. Pictured are (left to right) John McEleney, Mike Duea, Mike Clemons, Nick Nichols, Mark Birdnow, Scott Deter, Tom Fitzpatrick, Rusty Jones, Stan Moffitt, M.O. "Bud" Kahn, Allen Chapman, and Jack Scieszinski.

Chevrolet, Lowden. Kemmann Chevrolet, which started in 1875 by selling horse-drawn wagons, was featured in *AutoExec Magazine*, an NADA publication, for its 132 years of retailing.

Foundation

In 2001, a permanent endowed scholarship was established in the name of Foundation founder George White, Ames.

As the result of an IAD Foundation meeting in January, 2002, the association held a forum for automotive instructors at Iowa's community colleges to "identify ways to 'make the connection' between Iowa graduates and the new car and truck dealers of the state." The session was attended by teachers of auto technology, diesel technology, and collision repair at North Iowa Area Community College, Des Moines Area Community College, Indian Hills Community College, Southeast Iowa Community College, and Northwest Iowa Community College.

Now held annually, these meetings have resulted in an exchange of information on teaching policies, future business partnerships, and potential funding sources, as well as the creation of a Web site that allows instructors to communicate with each other more efficiently. Participants exchange ideas on how IADA can help students pursue careers in some aspect of the auto industry. This program continues to be valued by both

IADA and the community college instructors. "We're able to secure a much higher quality of employee thanks to the community college program," said Rich Willis, Willis Auto Campus, 2006 IADA chairman of the board.

A program by Safety Kleen benefited the IAD Foundation from 2003 to 2005. This vendor, specializing in parts cleaning and used oil pick-up, committed 10 cents per gallon of used oil collected to the IAD Foundation. The foundation received more than $6,000 to support youth educational training but discontinued the program in April, 2005, for lack of participation.

As of the 2007 annual meeting, the IAD Foundation raised more than $850,000 and awarded more than 140 scholarships. In 2007, the foundation awarded 14 scholarships of $1,425 each.

Trips Offered

While IADA no longer coordinates pre- or post-convention trips, the association since 2000 has offered numerous adventures for dealers through Global Holiday. These have included a Danube River Cruise, a Caribbean cruise, and trips to Prague, Vienna, Ireland, Switzerland, Austria, Paris, London, Rome, China, and Italy. In May, 2002, IADA members were invited to join Nebraska dealers at the Broadmoor in Colorado for that group's state convention.

National Statistics

For 2005, NADA reported that new car dealers in Iowa were responsible for 21.4 percent of all retail sales. The average sales per dealership was $16.0 million, and total sales of all new-vehicle dealerships in the state reached $6.3 billion. It was estimated that Iowa had 394 new-vehicle dealerships employing 12,628 for an annual payroll of $478 million.

In February of 2006, NADA membership was at an all-time high with more than 20,000 members representing more than 94 percent of franchised new-car dealers. In 2003, only one new car dealer in the state was not a member of IADA. The association had 385 franchised dealer members in 2007.

Gary Thomas and Stan Moffitt may look like a couple of kahunas residing in paradise, but they were together for the 2000 summer board meeting in Galena. "Some of the very best friends I've met in the IADA are the staff and employees of the association," said Moffitt.

In 2007, Lowden, Iowa, celebrated its sesquicentennial, and the oldest business in town was 132-year-old Kemmann Chevrolet, which opened its doors in 1875.

Donna and Don Meier appeared in Lowden's 2007 Sesquicentennial parade in the wood-bodied Orient Buckboard automobile purchased in 1904 by H.D. Kemmann. Don, the dealership's current owner, began working at the dealership in 1950.

1904
ORIENT

1854

H.D. Kemmann was born in Germany in 1854 and came to Iowa by way of Illinois, seeking work with a blacksmith. After four months of labor in Lowden, his employer couldn't pay him, so H.D. was given the blacksmith shop to settle the $80 debt of wages in 1875. He later purchased the building. H.D. Kemmann and Sons was born as a blacksmith and wagon shop.

1904

With three of his oldest sons (H.D. had eight sons, plus four daughters) Kemmann expanded the business to Clarence in 1904 to promote the sale of buggies and implements. One of those three sons, Paul, had a son named Cyrus who is the uncle-by-marriage of the current owner, Don Meier (Don's mother and Cyrus's wife were sisters). With the exception of his time in business school and the army, Meier has been employed at Kemmann since graduating from high school in 1950. In 1904 H.D. Kemmann took delivery of a wood-bodied Orient

Buckboard automobile for his personal use. That automobile was shipped in crates from Massachusetts, and its single-cylinder engine got more than 40 miles to the gallon. Over the years the dealership served as the agency for a variety of automobiles, including Marathon (1912), Ford (1913), Case (1914), Overland (1915), and Chalmers (1916). Kemmann also marketed an assortment of agricultural machinery—even washing machines and lawnmowers.

1921

The blacksmith business was sold off in 1921, although it operated through 1927 within the Kemmann's building. In 1923 Kemmann switched from selling Ford to Chevrolet and has sold Chevrolet exclusively ever since.

1938

When H.D. died in 1938, his son Paul and two of Paul's sons, Cyrus and Gerald, continued to run the Lowden store. To honor the impressive history, H.D.'s original Orient remains in a corner of the showroom, where blacksmith tools from the early shop also are on display.

Long before automobiles became part of the inventory, H.D. Kemmann and Sons operated as a blacksmith shop, marketed wagons and buggies, and sold farm implements.

Past Presidents
AND BOARD CHAIRMEN OF IADA

1919 — John Rude, Marshalltown

1920 — G.V. (Verne) Orr, Council Bluffs

1921 — H.J. Lytle, Burlington

1922 — E.L. MaKibben, Cedar Rapids

1923 — Dean Schooler, Des Moines

1924 — Dean Schooler, Des Moines

1925 — W.E. Wissler, Des Moines
(began November, 1924)

1926 — C.A. Bowers, Council Bluffs
(began November, 1926)

1928 — W.W. Sears, Des Moines

1929 — L.M. Millsap, Cedar Rapids

1930 — L.M. Millsap, Cedar Rapids

1931 — Ryal Miller, Sioux City

1932 — George Duffield, Des Moines

1933 — Frank Collord, Jr., Waterloo

1934 — J.H. Marston, Mason City

1935 — Floyd E. Hughes, Sr., Council Bluffs

1936 — C.A. Morris, Waterloo

1937 — R.H. Allen, Cedar Rapids

1938 — A.B. Chambers, Des Moines

1939 — Harry Wardell, Oelwein

1940 — Tom A. Coughlin, Davenport

1941 — Ben Sanders, Des Moines

1942 — Vern Nall, Iowa City (April)

1942 — Elmer B. Dunn, Des Moines (began October)

1943 — Walter Mahoney, Sioux City

1944 — Howard Sole, Des Moines

1945 — Frank Schierbrock, Davenport

1946 — Paul Pritchard, Mason City

1947 — Glenn O. Fletcher, Cedar Rapids

1948 — Byron C. Hawn, Waterloo

1949 — Vincent J. Neu, Sr., Davenport

1950 — R.N. Archie, Sidney

1951 — R.E. McCoy, Carroll

1952 — Chet Carmer, Centerville

1953 — L.E. Sinner, Greenfield

1954 — William C. Culver, Cedar Rapids

1955 — Lee A. Thomas, Burlington

1956 — William Cramblit, Jr., Ottumwa

1957 — E.E. Wheeler, Waterloo

1958 — Clyde J. Murray, Sioux City

1959 — Robert E. Bickelhaupt, Clinton

1960 — Don J. Cornelison, Atlantic

1961 — M.O. (Bud) Kahn, Newton

1962 — Frank D. Potts, Marengo

1963 — Karl Jorde, Osage

1964 — Howard R. Howlett, Des Moines

1965 — Norman P. Dunlap, Ames

1966 — Floyd Hughes, Jr., Council Bluffs

1967 — Dwight Burkhart, Independence

1968 — Lee Holt, Spencer

1969 — Marvin Hartwig, Iowa City

1970 — Gary Lilly, West Des Moines

1971 — Les Weber, Dubuque

1972 — Ray Lauterbach, Perry

1973 — Tom Helms, Davenport

1974 — Mert Coover, Nevada

1975 — Marvin Simpson, Newton

1976 — Wayne Johnson, Denison

1977 — H.E. Morrison, Jr., Stuart

1978 — Charlie Zook, Sioux City

1979 — W. H. (Bill) Perdock, Washington
1980 — Robert Schukei, Mason City
1981 — Edmund S. Elbert, Whittemore
1982 — Willard Loots, Marshalltown
1983 — Bob Axtell, Newton
1984 — John O. Falb, West Union
1985 — Dave Ostrem, Des Moines
1986 — Orv Roecker, Harlan
1987 — Leon Vaughn, Ottumwa
1988 — Dan McConnell, Waterloo
1989 — Wes Finch, Grinnell
1990 — Dick Dirks, Akron
1991 — Allen Chapman, Cedar Rapids
1992 — Harry McMullen, Council Bluffs
1993 — Roland Griffith, Carroll
1994 — Stew Hansen, Des Moines
1995 — Don Pierson, Spencer
1996 — Vinje Dahl, Davenport
1997 — Dan Kruse, Dubuque
1998 — Dean Beecher, Shenandoah
1999 — Rusty Jones, Manchester
2000 — Stan Moffitt, Boone
2001 — John McEleney, Clinton
2002 — Jim Hayden, Osage
2003 — Jack Scieszinski, Albia
2004 — Mark Birdnow, Jesup
2005 — Tom Fitzpatrick, Storm Lake
2006 — Rich Willis, Des Moines
2007 — Phil Weber, Dubuque
2008 — Bill Colwell, Hudson

In 1999 the IADA changed the title of its top volunteer leadership position from president to board chairman. Warren McEleney, NADA past president, is the only IADA honorary past chairman.

IADA
STAFF LEADERS

Andy Knapp—*May 1, 1919 to September, 1925; June, 1926–May, 1927*

T.W. (Tim) LeQuatte—*October, 1925 (served for less than one year)*

Walter Ferrell—*June, 1927–August, 1941*

Ray Spatz—*September, 1941–April, 1942*

V.E. Laurence—*October, 1942*
(no photo available)

George Means—*August, 1945–May, 1950*

Alfred W. Kahl—*September, 1950–October, 1981*

Gary Thomas—*Joined staff in 1980; named executive vice president in 1982*

Barber H.C. Hartwig signed on with Overland at the Iowa State Fair in 1912 and sold more than his initial 12-month allotment of 25 vehicles to lay the groundwork for Hartwig Motors.

Presidents' Stories

Marvin Hartwig

Marvin Hartwig, 1969 IADA president, can trace his family's automobile dealership back to John Hanson, the man who—as president of the Northeastern Iowa Automobile Dealers—brought together leading dealers to create IADA. Hartwig's father, Henry (H.C.) Hartwig, was a barber in Clutier, Iowa, who attended the Iowa State Fair in 1912. Hanson, a distributor of Overland Cars, had a display there and H.C. signed up to take 25 new Overlands during a 12-month period.

"Facilities weren't too important back then," says Marv Hartwig. The people of Clutier "thought H.C. was crazy for making such a commitment but by the end of the 12 months, he had sold in excess of his initial allotment and laid the foundation for Hartwig Motors Inc."

Mark Birdnow

When he was a year out of high school, 18-year-old **Mark Birdnow** decided that he could sell cars. "I applied for a couple of openings in the paper, but was barely given the time of day," says Birdnow, IADA's president in 2004. "In those days nearly all car salespeople were male, over 30, and white. I looked like a kid and that was a big concern to those who were interviewing me. As I passed by an AMC dealer in Cedar Falls, I thought, *I love my Gremlin (my first car). I can certainly sell something I like so much.* So I pulled in and asked for a job.

"I had to call back three times, but after pestering them they finally acquiesced. I remember the dealer had to call his attorney to see if I could sign the bottom of the sales order as the dealers 'authorized representative,' as I wasn't of legal age yet. After four and a half years, I thought I was ready to be a dealer (my, how little I really knew) and purchased a very small AMC dealership in my hometown of Oelwein in 1976. I was told that I was the youngest AMC dealer in the country.

"Starting with nothing and no family members in the business, I've been able to build a business that includes six auto-related businesses. It became a true family business. ... My sons have what it will take to be future dealers, and that is what is most gratifying to me." Birdnow owns Mark Birdnow Chevrolet in Jesup and Birdnow Motor Trade in Oelwein.

Allen Chapman

Allen Motor Company of Cedar Rapids traces its beginnings to 1903. **Ray Allen** was president of IADA in 1937. Nephew Allen Chapman, who joined the company in the mid-1960s, was IADA president in 1991 and won the Time Magazine Quality Dealer Award in 1996.

In 1913 the staff of Allen Brothers included William Allen, Bert Matthews, Oley Allen, Albert Allen and Ray Allen.

John Falb, Jr.

John Falb, Jr., IADA's 1984 president, was the youngest of the four sons who became part of John Falb & Sons of Elgin, Iowa. The company sold 34 cars in 1912, its first year. Brothers George, Walter and Herbert joined the company in the 1920s. John Falb, Jr., joined the firm in 1931 and was in charge of the Postville branch. On its 20ᵗʰ anniversary in 1932, the company served northeast Iowa from Elgin, Postville, and Clermont.

Clinton's McEleneys Make First Father & Son Team to Lead NADA

In 2009, Iowa will be part of a national auto-industry first. Clinton auto dealers Warren and John McEleney, mentioned previously in this book, will become the first father and son to serve as the top elected leaders of the National Automobile Dealers Association.

Warren McEleney was NADA president in 1972 and his son, John, is slated to become chairman of the prestigious group in 2009. Both served as NADA directors for IADA. John served as IADA's chairman, and Warren is the only honorary president of IADA, having never served a term in the state association's top chair.

When Warren was NADA president, President Nixon was struggling to get a grip on inflation, and the big issue was the national economy. Warren attended the bill-signing for legislation that enacted price controls on many consumer goods. Both NADA and its president from Iowa were proud that automobiles were excluded from price controls.

John believes the major issues in the future will be the profitability of dealerships, impact of new political influences in Washington, restructuring of domestic manufacturers, and economic challenges, including escalating oil prices that will require dealers to adapt to new consumer demands.

While more than 35 years will separate their terms at the helm of NADA, Warren and John feel that NADA's commitment to the dealer body has not changed. Some 500 NADA employees work to limit legislation that would negatively impact the automobile industry, continually dialogue with manufacturers, and assist the dealer membership in making their businesses more profitable.

NOTE: The McEleney family's involvement in IADA dates to Warren's father, Leo McEleney, who in 1921 began serving as the Clinton County member on the Iowa Motor Trades board. While he never served as state president, Leo McEleney founded McEleney Auto Company with his brother, E.J., a machinist, in 1914. Leo was just 20 years old. The bulletin read: "Leo states that at the time he had but $75, but that he was able to secure a loan through a local bank sufficient to enable him to take a half interest in the business." Leo went on to serve in the Iowa Legislature, always remaining a champion of the needs of Iowa's auto dealers.

Warren and John McEleney are the first father and son combination to win election to the top leadership role within the National Automobile Dealers Association. Thirty-seven years separate their terms.

146　　　IOWA TODAY

G. H. Falb

John Falb
General Manager

W. C. Falb

CHEVROLET

SALES AND SERVICE

AN INSTITUTION FOUNDED ON COURTESY AND SERVICE
DEDICATED TO THE MOTOR VEHICLE NEEDS
OF NORTHEASTERN IOWA.

JOHN FALB & SONS

ELGIN, IOWA

Northeast Iowa's Used Car Market

H. W. Falb

John Jr. Falb

Ad Credit—Iowa Today, School Necessities Company, Marquette, Iowa, 1931

TIME Magazine's Quality Dealer Award
RECIPIENTS FROM IOWA

The TIME Magazine Quality Dealer Award is the auto industry's most prestigious and highly coveted award for car dealers. TMQDA recipients, who are among the most successful dealers in the nation, also have demonstrated a long-standing commitment to community service. The TIME Magazine award is sponsored in association with Goodyear and in cooperation with NADA.

IOWA DEALERS WHO HAVE BEEN HONORED ARE:

Clyde J. Murray—*1960, Finalist*
   (Benjamin Franklin Quality Dealer Award)
Charles Betts, Jr., Des Moines—*1969*
Ray Lauterbach, Perry—*1972,*
   Regional Winner/Finalist
Lee Holt, Spencer—*1973*
Floyd Hughes, Council Bluffs—*1974*
Marvin Hartwig, Iowa City—*1975,*
   Regional Winner/Finalist
Charlie Zook, Sioux City—*1976*
Warren McEleney, Clinton—*1977,*
   National Winner
Leo Levien, Fort Dodge—*1978*
Gary Lilly, West Des Moines—*1979*
Art Salsness, Sioux City—*1980*
Tom Helms, Davenport—*1981*
Bill Percock, Washington—*1982,*
   Regional Winner/Finalist
Eddie Elbert, Whittemore—*1983,*
   Regional Winner/Finalist
Mert Coover, Nevada—*1984*
John O. Falb, West Union—*1985,*
   Regional Winner/Finalist
Dave Ostrem, Des Moines—*1986*

Orv Roecker, Harlan—*1987*
Bob Axtell, Newton—*1988*
Leon Vaughn, Ottumwa—*1989*
Bill Fletcher, Cedar Rapids—*1990*
Charles Betts, Jr., Des Moines—*1991,*
   Regional Winner/Finalist
Wes Finch, Grinnell—*1992*
Pete Pohlmann, Davenport—*1993,*
   Regional Winner/Finalist
Stan Moffitt, Boone—*1994*
Dan Kruse, Dubuque—*1995*
Allen Chapman, Cedar Rapids—*1996*
Harry McMullen, Council Bluffs—*1997*
John Keady, Davenport—*1998*
Charlie Zook, Sioux City—*1999, National Winner*
Charles Gabus, Des Moines—*2000*
John Deery, Sr., Cedar Falls—*2001*
John Schroeder, Bloomfield—*2002*
Bill Jensen, Des Moines—*2003*
Mark Birdnow, Jesup—*2004*
Stew Hansen, Des Moines—*2005*
Rich Willis, Des Moines—*2006*
Dale Howard, Iowa Falls—*2007*
Casey Johnson, Fort Dodge—*2008*

Hall of Fame
INSTITUTED IN 2008

To honor a lifetime and career dedicated to excellence in Iowa's automobile industry, IADA created a Hall of Fame in 2008. Induction of the inaugural class took place on April 11, 2008, and those celebrated and honored were Edmund S. Elbert (posthumously), John O. Falb, Marvin Hartwig, Warren McEleney, and Charlie Zook.

Hall of Fame inductees must have exhibited exemplary performance in the areas of leadership, mentoring, and personal commitment and contribution both within and outside the auto industry.

Hall of Fame membership is limited to association members who have served the industry in at least three of the following major positions:
- NADA president/chairperson
- NADA director from Iowa
- IADA president/chairperson
- IADA insurance management board chairperson
- DEAC/ICAR chairperson
- IAD Foundation for Education president
- National winner or finalist of the Time Magazine Quality Dealer of the Year/Iowa Dealer of the Year Award
- National winner or finalist of the Truck Dealer of the Year Award
- American Truck Dealer chairperson

Other persons in the industry whose distinguished performances are worthy of the award will also be considered for induction by the IADA Executive Committee. Nominees are eligible for IADA Hall of Fame selection two years after they meet the minimum requirements. One individual will now be inducted every three years as part of the annual meeting of IADA.

HALF CENTURY HALF OF FAME

1984

**Original inductees present
at the 1984 convention:**

Bentley Chevrolet, Fairbank
Braga Motor Company, Marshalltown
Buckwalter Motors Inc., Wellman
Burns Motor Company, Spirit Lake
E.M. Christensen Auto Company, Harlan
Bob Coonradt Ford-Mercury, Waverly
Danielson Motor Company, Fairfield
Dau's Garage, Algona
Dirks Motor Company, Akron
John Falb Company, West Union
Glover Motor Company, Ottumwa
Hartwig Motors, Iowa City
Marv Hartwig Inc., Iowa City
Hollander Motor, Inc., Schleswig
Huinker Chevrolet, Monona
Kemmann Chervolet, Lowden
Godfrey Klimesh Motor Sales, Calmar
Morrison Chevrolet Company, Stuart
Munsen Chevrolet-Buick, Story City
Read Auto Company, Stanhope
Schukei Chevrolet, Mason City
Simmons Motor Company, Marengo
Torkelson Motors, Inc., Elgin
F.E. Welterlen Motors, Edgewood
Vaughn Chevrolet, Ottumwa

**Qualified for induction but unable
to attend 1984 convention:**

William Ambrose Auto Company, Tripoli
Bissonnette Chevrolet, Charles City
I.W. Braga & Sons, Iowa Falls
Bruesewitz Chervolet, Grafton
Buhr Chevrolet-Buick, Tripoli
Carr Chevrolet, Milford
Crescent Chevrolet, Des Moines

Grovert Motor Company, Newhall
Kewin Auto Company, Griswold
Koehn Motor Company, Victor
Mitchell Motor Company, Adel
Herb Moffitt's Inc., Boone
Jack Morris Motors, Centerville
Mouw Motor Company, Sioux Center
Olesen Chevrolet-Olds, Avoca
Pews Inc., LeMars
Rasmussen Motor Sales, Maquoketa
Riha Auto Sales, Vining
Schuelke Auto Company, Storm Lake
Spoerl Chevrolet, Sherrill
Tegeler's Inc., Dubuque
Weis Buick-AMC, Decorah
Whiteis Auto Company, Forest City
McEleney Motors, Clinton

1985

Anderson-Weber, Dubuque
Ulrich Motor Company, Pella
Mills Motor Company, Winterset
Pritchard Auto Company, Britt
Allen Motor Company, Cedar Rapids

1986

Donovan Motors, Inc., Estherville
Ervin Motor Company, Vinton
White Motor Company, Lamoni
Wilhite International and Pontiac, Keswick
Fisher-Pont Inc., Stratford

1987

Kingland Motor Co., Lake Mills
Schwind Boeker, Inc., Davenport
Taylor Motor Sales, Olin
Rex Chevrolet, Odebolt
Erdmann Motor Co., Osage
Koehn Motor Co., Vinton

1988

Strieter Motors, Davenport
Raleigh Johnson Motor Co., Belle Plaine
Ley Motor, Lakota

1989

Beneventi Chevrolet, Granger
Cass Motors Inc., Onawa
Peterson Motor Company, Storm Lake
Howard Shimon Inc, Pocahontas
Ver Hoef Chevrolet Inc., Sioux Center
Hummel's Nissan, Des Moines
Kramer Auto Sales, New Hampton
Christensen Motor Co., Eagle Grove
Hutchinson Chevrolet-Olds, Inc., Onawa
Bradley Auto Sales, Decorah
Norman Brothers, Primghar

1990s

Dahms Chevrolet, Donnellson
Hoak Motors, Sioux City
K&W Motors, New Hampton
McCarville & Sons, Carroll
Clinton Lincoln-Mercury, Clinton
Sedars Motor Company, Mason City.

2000s

Mikels, Inc., Bloomfield
Albia Motor Co., Albia
Shore Motor Company, Clarinda
Handel-Rotman Motor Company, Maquoketa
Shaull & Ullerich, Blairstown
Duea Motor Company, Albia
McGrath Automotive Group, Cedar Rapids
Clark Chevrolet, LaPorte City
Charles Gabus Ford, Des Moines
Harvey Brothers Olds-GMC (Original name for
    Glendenning Motor Company)
Mt. Ayr Miller Chevrolet, Corning
Nesselroad Chevrolet, Brooklyn
Rouse Motor Company, Grundy Center

Ken Wise Buick, Marshalltown
Elbert Chevrolet, Whittemore
Keast Chevrolet Olds Pontiac, Oakland
Kemna Motor Company, Bancroft
McCormick Motors, Ida Grove

75 YEAR HALL OF FAME

1990s

Kemmann Chevrolet of Lowden
Kingland Motor Co., Lake Mills
Olesen Chevrolet, Avoca
Schallau Motor Co., Van Horne

2000s

Buhr Chevrolet, Tripoli
J.M. Jones & Son, Inc., Manchester
Torkelson Motors, Elgin
Mouw Motor Company, Sioux City
H&N Chevrolet, Spencer
Huinker Garage, Monona
Hummel's Nissan, Des Moines
Ogden Motor Company, Ogden
    (now Moffitt's Inc. of Boone)
Spoerl Chevrolet, Sherrill
Pritchard Auto Co., Garner, Britt and Forest City
Ervin Motors, Vinton
Schuelke Auto Company, Storm Lake
Beneventi Chevrolet, Granger
Schukei Chevrolet, Mason City
Vollmar Motors, Holstein

CENTURY OF SERVICE

2000s

Allen Motor Company, Cedar Rapids
    (originally Elkader)
Kemmann Chevrolet, Lowden

Acknowledgments

Thank you to the following individuals and businesses who contributed memories, photos and other memorabilia for the IADA history project:

AUTO DEALERS

Allen Motor Company
Anderson-Weber, Inc.
Birdnow GM Dealerships
Bob Brown Chevrolet, Inc.
Crescent Chevrolet, Inc.
Grovert Motor Company
Hartwig Motors, Inc.
Holmes Imports
Hummel's Nissan
Kemmann Chevrolet
Kemna Motor Company
Knoepfler Chevrolet
Lauterbach Buick-Pontiac
Lou Walsh Motors
McEleney Motors, Inc.
McCarville & Son Motor Co., Inc.
Rotman Motor Company, Inc.
Schukei Chevrolet, Inc.
Streiter Lincoln Mercury/Strieter River City Ford
White Way Auto Company

INDIVIDUALS

Lee Aldermann
Bob Axtell, Jr.
Brad Braga and Braga family members
Nancy Whitley-Coates
Bill Colwell
The Family of Eddie Elbert
Dave Esbeck
Marv Hartwig
Pauline Hazen, Louise Bos and Enid Phillips
Grace Huffman
M.O. "Bud" Kahn
Glenda Millard
Steve Mores
Bruce Nelsen
William J. Peverill
Glenn Summers
Leland Thornburg
Mark Wetmore
Carl Wohlenberg
John Worden

OTHERS

The Des Moines Register
Ottumwa Courier
Mason City Globe Gazette
State Historical Society of Iowa